Andrea—

I'm honored by you .... you could
hopefully there are some stories or ideas you find
useful. It's been wonderful getting to know you,
and I'm proud to be your teammate!

Jason Randell

"Having met many great leaders in my career, I can say with certainty that Jason is one of the few who can actually 'do it all.' This book is appropriate and good advice for anyone in leadership because even though you just might be able to 'do it all,' you shouldn't. Jason outlines pitfalls and how to avoid them while building an organization that can thrive during the good and bad times. Great advice on how to stay humble and transparent and be an even better leader."

—Kevin Stadler

CEO, Evolon Technology

"Jason drives home an important point for every emerging leader (and a great reminder for veteran business leaders): your greatest successes will happen when you build a strong team both inside and outside your organization. Better yet, he shares the mindset and the tools necessary to help attract and develop that team."

—Jim O'Connor

National Practice Leader, PEO and Association Consulting, CBIZ Benefits and Insurance Services

"Jason has been a confidant and adviser to me from the moment I first met him because he's smart as a whip and has clarity around some of the thorniest issues facing executives these days. His book is filled with stories of his own leadership path and the wisdom he uncovered along the way. It's a very authentic, easily digestible guide to leadership success."

—Jim Cascino

CEO and President, Eos International (retired)

"Jason is one of my closest friends and most valued colleagues. Almost always the smartest guy in any room, I know Jason still had to earn (often the hard way) the wisdom he's able to share in this fantastic and necessary book. The idea of 'executive exceptionalism' as a trap is brilliantly insightful, and I agree that it is as common as it is misguided. Beyond the Superhero *is keenly perceptive and emotionally vulnerable, but also tactically useful. It should be required reading for all new CEOs—or any new leader who feels alone at the top."*

—Matthew Harris

President, US Cloud

"The myth of the all-knowing CEO is just that: a myth. Unfortunately, it is a harmful myth, as too many leaders attempt to operate in a fashion they imagine those 'iconic and heroic leaders' appear to. Jason points out that the CEO's primary job is to build a terrific culture and simplify communication and decision-making at their company. This story makes me think back to my father's early advice to me: you have two ears and one mouth, so use them in that proportion. Following Jason's story will help set your organization up for a vastly better chance of success."

—Gary Noke

President and CEO, PrismHR

"No leader can—or should—try to do it all. Jason's wit and wisdom shine through in a work that will make you a better, happier leader today. And his advice will set your organization up for spectacular success."

—Stephanie Harris

President, Incentive Research Foundation

BEYOND THE
SUPERHERO

JASON RANDALL

BEYOND THE SUPERHERO

EXECUTIVE LEADERSHIP FOR THE REST OF US

ForbesBooks

Published by ForbesBooks, Charleston, South Carolina.
Member of Advantage Media Group.

ForbesBooks is a registered trademark, and the ForbesBooks colophon is a trademark of Forbes Media, LLC.

Printed in the United States of America.

10 9 8 7 6 5 4 3 2 1

ISBN: 978-1-950863-20-4
LCCN: 2021900512

Cover design by Megan Elger.
Layout design by Mary Hamilton.

This custom publication is intended to provide accurate information and the opinions of the author in regard to the subject matter covered. It is sold with the understanding that the publisher, Advantage|ForbesBooks, is not engaged in rendering legal, financial, or professional services of any kind. If legal advice or other expert assistance is required, the reader is advised to seek the services of a competent professional.

 Advantage Media Group is proud to be a part of the Tree Neutral® program. Tree Neutral offsets the number of trees consumed in the production and printing of this book by taking proactive steps such as planting trees in direct proportion to the number of trees used to print books. To learn more about Tree Neutral, please visit **www.treeneutral.com**.

Since 1917, Forbes has remained steadfast in its mission to serve as the defining voice of entrepreneurial capitalism. ForbesBooks, launched in 2016 through a partnership with Advantage Media Group, furthers that aim by helping business and thought leaders bring their stories, passion, and knowledge to the forefront in custom books. Opinions expressed by ForbesBooks authors are their own. To be considered for publication, please visit **www.forbesbooks.com**.

To the entrepreneur. The new executive. The up-and-comer eager to leave an impact and, in time, a legacy. I hope my words can inspire and guide you as you work with your team to build something special.

CONTENTS

FOREWORD

I am honored to provide a foreword to this quite useful and topical book. Author Jason Randall is a friend whose career progress and successes I have long admired, and I have also witnessed him on the naturally winding road that many of us experience getting from point A to our goals. You may enjoy his mention of being a pizza franchise owner. My family and I flipped pizzas in what was then his store on a fun and celebrated weekend many years ago! Jason's intelligence, determination, confidence, and overall can-do attitude have served him well. He provides us with great food for thought in this book. *Beyond the Superhero* has most immediately aided me in even preparing this foreword.

I am Doug Rubenstein, husband to the love of my life, who is also my high school sweetheart from over forty years ago; proud father of two phenomenal sons currently in the early years of their respective careers; and hopefully the best patriarch I can be for my family. Putting my heart and soul into my family and friends continually reinforces the foundation from which I challenge myself to put an equal degree into my career. In my mind, it can all come full circle as the treasured color and intensity of life.

Beyond the Superhero guides leaders to the long view. Many talk about the journey, the perseverance, and the tenacity needed to pace oneself while leading. My mom was an artist, and we are fortunate to have many of her works treasured in our home. Included are two oil paintings of the same Waterloo Bridge in London. One was painted by my mom when she was age seventeen. The other was painted by her when she was age seventy-seven. In one, the sun is rising; in the other, the sun is setting. The two works share a bridge of sixty years. Mustering up the long perspective and endurance is part of leadership that can create ageless and timeless success. Artistic success requires zeal, which is the product of creativity and energy. There is a romantic combination of leadership and art that can empower you to live dreams and build.

As to building business, I am currently the chief operating officer, a board member, and an investor for Benjamin F. Edwards, a full-service broker dealer and RIA in the financial wealth management industry with a legacy spanning over 130 years and five generations of the Edwards family. We are privately held, independent, and owned by employees, family, and friends of the firm. My career with Edwards, as we proudly and simply refer to it, spans over thirty years, and for that I am truly blessed. I report directly to my dear friend Tad Edwards, our founder, chairman, CEO, and president. I am also the current independent chairman of the board of CatchMark Timber Trust, a NYSE-listed REIT based in Atlanta that engages in timberland ownership and management. I first associated with CatchMark as a director at its IPO in late 2013. Both of these leadership roles provide countless business and personal life lessons. Living actively and concurrently with family, friends, and business is thrilling and a dream come true.

It is all about "we" in the success of our business, yet I will admit that it takes a lot of "me" calling upon "myself" behind the scenes to dig deep, including those proverbial and really lonely times on certain days and nights. Edwards lives by intrinsic goals that have created the wiring within me and our team. Our shared values are woven deeply. And I'm so glad to see that these shared values that "we" and "I" have found so essential also figure so prominently in Jason's work.

I am deeply thankful for mentors. Time with a mentor is like a good cup of coffee or a great glass of wine. You know and feel the experience when you see it. Mentors can supercharge the "me" so that leaders can confidently and trustingly be in the thick of it with the "we." There isn't a day in which I don't ask myself what one of my mentors would say or think about my performance.

I was mesmerized as a young kid with the little red wagon given to me by the most special of mentors in my life, Norman Handel. Norman was my father's boss, who became my parents' best friend to such an exalted level that they referred to him as my godfather. He was a father and a teacher. It is through Norman that I had the great fortune of meeting the Edwards family. Norman grew up during the Great Depression, and that formed his work ethic. And Norman helped form my similar work ethic.

My mom, also a grandly significant mentor, taught me to metaphorically put all the good stuff I experience in life in that wagon. She would always say to "remember the good stuff." I often ask coworkers, friends, and family, "What's in your wagon?" Sharing what is in *your* wagon can communicate certain ideas and goals to your business teams, your family, and your friends.

The management goals in my little red wagon come from experiencing, living, and learning and include, from Edwards:

- putting clients' interests first and striving to exceed their expectations;

- being values-driven, mission-centric, and culturally aligned;

- grounding yourself and your company in the Golden Rule, treating others the way you want to be treated;

- knowing and acting upon "What is your why?"

- having fun and wholeheartedly celebrating successes along every step of the journey.

From my mom:

- being genuine and sincere, kind and caring, and being intentionally present;

- being a passionate business artist; and

- doing so such that you will be proud of yourself and those special to you will be proud as well.

From Norman:

- accomplishing more with sugar than with salt;

- working humbly and feverishly;

- taking nothing for granted and earning every bit of what you have.

Much of what is in my little red wagon speaks to Jason's work as well, in particular the chapter on servant leadership.

It is a chapter that speaks closely to leading with passion, intensity, and purpose, and provides the fundamentals of leading with care and advocacy. The chapter emphasizes that the outward motivation of "we" is what's introspectively calling upon the "me."

I hope you enjoy the read as I did, perhaps with some good coffee and great wine.

—Doug Rubenstein

Chief Operating Officer, Benjamin F. Edwards & Co.; Chairman of the Board, CatchMark Timber Trust (NYSE: CTT)

INTRODUCTION

Just after my thirty-fourth birthday, I became CEO of a rocket ship of a company that operated as Coast to Coast Tickets, selling sports, entertainment, and other event tickets online. It was a pleasure until sales suddenly crashed in 2006. I will never forget waking up in the morning and feeling fine for only a few seconds before a heavy weight of anxiety would land on me. My company was in mortal danger, and I was responsible for saving it.

Looking back at that short-lived business crisis, I realize that I had fallen for what this book will call the CEO superhero myth. I am recounting here in great candor what I have learned leading corporate teams big and small because I know from experience the emotional challenges inherent in leadership. Taking over a top executive office and dealing with inevitable crises can be immensely overwhelming, and we must honestly admit that we can't do it alone.

It did not take long to discover why ticket orders abruptly fell off at Coast to Coast. The e-commerce company started a few years earlier by my brother, Mike Randall, was a one-trick pony with a very good trick. There was one reason it had grown rapidly to employ a couple dozen people and had just moved into a new building. It was attracting around a million visitors per month to a website that was adept at making itself easy to find through online search. We were in a very good place, but we knew we were vulnerable to being displaced at any moment. Google and other big tech companies make the rules governing online search, specifically the algorithms that determine who is relevant and who is invisible. These giants can and do change the rules without warning.

One day typing "Chicago Bears tickets" or tens of thousands of other search terms was likely to turn up our website at or near the top of the list. The next day we were off the screen. That's equivalent to having a roadside motel on the highway and waking up one day to find the highway gone.

Because we had multiple appearances on the *Inc.* 500 list of fastest-growing companies, we attracted a lot of interest from venture capital and private equity firms. We were looking for ways to expand and solidify the business, in light of our search-engine vulnerability. Just four days before our search terms crashed, I was on a high floor of a fancy office building near Beverly Hills, staring at an original Modigliani painting as a venture capital partner presented me with a term sheet that valued our highly profitable business well into eight figures. We were being celebrated as a key player in our niche industry with the brightest future ahead of us. One week later, we needed to calculate how many days it would be before we couldn't make payroll. On a personal level, I went from imagining a lucrative, life-changing buyout to worrying about putting food on the table. That memory sticks with you.

My brother had hired me to help manage the company's growth, and I had no expertise in search engine optimization or computer coding. But my team had those specialists. Through trial and error and persistence, they were able to get our search terms back to functioning as well as or better than before. After a couple of weeks, our growth resumed, our one-trick pony was again prancing around the virtual paddock, and the story had a happy ending. That was a different time, when a small company without an established brand had a greater chance to perform well on search terms. The technical nature of business challenges will always change over time, but this book is about more abiding truths. What got me through the crisis and many more to come was staying positive, staying focused, and displaying an outward calm and a confidence in the team.

I told the employees that, to be honest, I didn't know whether our business was recoverable, but if it was, I was sure that we had the exact right people to do it. Projecting a fundamental sense of optimism, without being a Pollyanna, the message was, "I believe in you. I believe in us. Let's build a bright future together."

This book is intended to provide an expanded version of that same message to senior executives. We are in a position in which the floor could drop out from under us at any time. We are always facing huge new challenges that we are not prepared for. We must live with a feeling that our next decision could be our last in our current position. But the central premise of this book is optimistic, not fatalistic: with authenticity and humility, we can keep the energy aloft and build great results.

By now you may have figured out where this leadership book is coming from philosophically—that building and serving our team is the starting point. The platitude about leadership is that it's lonely at the top. But does it have to be? I'm inviting you to come along with me as I explore that question. Most of us can't fathom the challenges of leadership until our first major leadership role. Perhaps you got a long-awaited promotion you had been working toward your whole life. Or maybe it was unexpected, as when someone too suddenly inherits a family business. Even if you achieved your position by methodically demonstrating your abilities, capacity, and innovative ideas, your talent and ambition are not going to keep you from feeling overwhelmed. What I am sharing here, which I believe all veteran leaders would confirm if they are honest about their feelings, is that in the early days, weeks, months, and sometimes years, we're going to feel like we're completely out of our depth.

In fact, no matter how much time we spend in leadership, we're always going to face new challenges as we set a new target, take on a new role, or turn the page on a new chapter in our organization's story. These new challenges may leave us feeling daunted or isolated while others are looking toward us for direction. Or even worse, they may be looking away from us, the dramatic and challenging situation I describe in chapter 1.

CHAPTER ONE

IN THE EYE OF THE STORM

One winter Friday in early 2018, I started a new job, and like every new job I've had, it was nothing like what I was accustomed to. I was being introduced as the new CEO of Questco in a situation that was the epitome of awkwardness. I had been working in the same business sector as Questco—the outsourcing of human resources—but was frightened by how little I knew about what I was walking into. You could say that I was addressing an assembly room full of strangers, but it was worse than that.

Questco's original office space, which it had been in for twenty-nine years, consisted of a couple of rundown buildings in Conroe, Texas, that weren't that nice when they were new. And they were really far from new. People in Houston might consider Conroe a distant suburb with piney woods and recreational lakes, but this part of Conroe was by some railroad tracks that didn't have a right side. If your dentist chose that location, you'd want to find a different dentist. There were feral cats in the parking lot, dead armadillos on the road, and probably drug dealers working out of the service station parking lot across the street. The ramshackle office space had no meeting room that could hold our more than a hundred employees. So three or four dozen people piled into a narrow break room, wedged in between the ice machine and the bulk recycle bin, while about twenty others spilled out into the hallway, and the rest presumably listened from their desks or dialed in from remote locations to hear their new CEO being introduced.

Questco is a great company that I will be telling you more about as we explore together the challenges of executive leadership. But when I took over, the private equity firm that owned Questco had determined that it needed to grow—a lot. I was recruited using a retained search firm, so my hiring happened in almost complete secrecy from the viewpoint of the assembled managers and employees I was addressing. (In retained search, a recruiter gets an exclusive paid contract to conduct a search and present a short list of candidates who meet the criteria, usually for a senior position. This type of search is more rigorous and confidential than when executive recruiters work on a contingency basis, getting paid when or if their candidate gets a position.) During the interview process, I was allowed nowhere near the sad-looking "corporate campus" where the previous CEO had remained on the job until about twenty-four hours before my arrival.

I had gotten the job offer at the end of 2017 and promptly gave notice to my employer, Insperity. That large public company is a premium provider of HR outsourcing. Its office space a few miles down the road was a campus of high-rise buildings with fountains and marble and nice executive boardrooms. Questco was at that time less than 5 percent of Insperity's size by most measures.

When I stepped onto the mismatched wood laminate flooring of Questco's dingy break room, I knew the people I would be addressing had been through quite a bit of change already. The current owners had taken over about a year and a half earlier from a different private equity firm that was not around for long. Longtime employees of what once had been a folksy, family-owned firm had endured two quick flips and a lot of corporatization in a very short period. Now they were getting a leader from their big, bad competitor down the road. And this change was a total surprise to them because the departing CEO had very recently led off-site meetings to make strategic plans for the year.

In my hands I held an embossed black leather portfolio, newly purchased for my fresh start. The yellow notepad tucked into the houndstooth lining had been used only once, to write a single page of bullet points for a short speech. I started by thanking the CFO, Wendy, and our chairman, Nick, for their nice introductory remarks. Then I immediately acknowledged my predecessor, honoring his contribution, while having no idea how the people in front of me regarded him. I didn't know who his allies were, who his detractors were, or how anyone felt about his abrupt termination. But it was important to acknowledge an emotional change and that some of my audience might be missing him. As important, I believed that what I communicated about the prior CEO also signaled to my new team who I was as a person and as a leader.

What I said that morning was a step toward building a team at Questco, but it was also a step in the learning process that I am inviting readers to join me on in this book. I was trying to give a triumphant and motivating speech, but I didn't really have a good grasp of the challenge ahead. What I had been told, and what I believed, was that I was joining a healthy, well-functioning operation that just needed more of a sales leadership presence at the top to reach its growth potential and the investors' goals. I was being coronated to fill that leadership role. In the pages ahead, you'll see how my view of the challenge and my understanding of executive leadership evolved as reality set in.

In my remarks that morning, I recounted how I was introduced to what some call the professional employer organization (PEO) industry as a client. Taking advantage of outsourcing HR services to a provider like Questco, I was able to grow my company faster and to realize a lot of my personal and professional goals more quickly and effectively.

"People like you have changed my life," I said, "and that's why I feel so strongly about this industry, because we are in the business of helping business owners succeed. And that is such a powerful place to be, to offer that support. With us, those business owners don't feel alone."

Looking out at the dozens of strangers who now were my teammates, as well as the ones around the corner and on the phone whose reactions I couldn't see, I launched into the motivational section of the speech.

"But ultimately it's not about me and my goals. It's about us and the opportunity before us. And it's about writing the next chapter of the Questco growth story. And that growth creates fantastic opportunities for anyone who's within earshot of my voice. And each of you, and each member of your team, has a key part to play in this story."

What I believed then and went on to say was that our potential to retain clients and to grow would depend on decisions we would make over the next several weeks. I promised to inform myself by spending time with them and with key customers and other stake-holders before filling in the details of my plans for the company. And, in fact, that's what I did. But although I was promising a plan they could all get excited about, I didn't know how many of them were actually on their way out the door, or why. I'll explain that turnover later, but for now I'll just say that it didn't result from what I said next in my speech.

I addressed company culture, saying that as important as what we'd be doing is how we'd be doing it. "What kind of culture are we looking to build, develop, and nurture here?" I asked rhetorically. My answer involved four key attributes: simplicity, authenticity, electricity, and accountability.

We'll get back to these touchstones in chapter 3, but here is how I summarized them in my short speech:

Simplicity: Our HR outsourcing industry is built on a fundamental challenge. Our promise to our clients is that outsourcing their human resources responsibilities to us will make their lives easier. We are agreeing to take on tasks that multiple clients find too complex, costly, or burdensome to handle, and we must make that process look easy. We can accomplish that feat only by speaking directly to one another in a straightforward way so that what's expected of each of us is clear and consistent day-to-day.

Authenticity: Individually, each of us must be honest in our communications, and collectively, we must discuss what we do

> **"What kind of culture are we looking to build, develop, and nurture here?" I asked rhetorically. My answer involved four key attributes: simplicity, authenticity, electricity, and accountability.**

outwardly in the marketplace in a way that rings true to who we are and the unique value we can provide.

Electricity: An organization that can move at lightning speed, spark our interest, and fuel our motivation in ways that we find personally relevant is a fun and exciting place to work. We can celebrate progress and success and quickly pivot away from anything that happens to not be working.

Accountability: We hold ourselves and each other accountable for the success of our clients and by extension our company. Every goal has a measurement, and we manage, communicate, and report by the numbers.

I closed my remarks by saying, "As I enter this new environment, I'm extending trust to you in advance. I hope that you are willing to do the same and that I will earn your trust in time. And there's never been a better time to be part of our organization." Sounds confident, doesn't it? To be truthful, I was bewildered, scared, and disoriented. I didn't know what I was walking into or what was expected of me. Remember, I couldn't even see the faces of dozens of these strangers I was talking to. I didn't know where they were coming from, where their heads were at. Although I had been working in the same industry, Questco had not been in my line of sight given my specific responsibilities at Insperity. Also, Questco focused historically on a smaller and more blue-collar business clientele.

This book is about executive leadership, not about any particular industry. But because I will be referencing Questco for real-life examples, let me fill in some details about its business. It is owned by Parallel49 Equity, which is based in the Chicago area and invests in profitable, well-managed, lower middle market companies in the United States and Canada. Although private equity has a reputation for being numbers driven, Parallel49 is genuinely interested in building a great business and taking care of its people. An ownership that values the humanity of its team was central to my accepting the position at Questco. It would be hard to market your company as a great provider of human resources if you couldn't show that you cared about your own people. And what we do at Questco is not only taking over the mechanics of a client's HR administration or payroll functions but also handling the full range of human resources work for the client company.

A LEGACY OF PROMISES

Leaders in business, like those in politics, sometimes make promises they can't keep. I discovered during my early days at Questco that during the previous ownerships, many employees had built up certain expectations or received promises, generally not in writing, regarding their compensation or advancement opportunities. Some of the longest-serving employees had started when Questco was a close-knit family business, and they were used to a more informal management style than afforded by private equity ownership. Getting a new leader from a much larger corporation struck them as a harbinger of more of the change they already dreaded. Quite a few Questco employees felt some combination of disenchantment, exhaustion, betrayal, or at least skepticism. I am not blaming them, because they were genuinely nice people who had been through a lot. While my bright-eyed and bushy-tailed speech generated no discernible reaction, my follow-up conversations with individuals and small groups went well. Employees were eager to show me what they were doing, but the exhaustion and frustration had already taken its toll.

My hiring became a catalyst for a surprising number of long-term employees to say, "OK, I'm done here." They were yearning for a fresh start—somewhere else. I heard messages like "I love this place, and you seem awesome, but I just can't do this anymore." It reached the point that whenever an employee said to me, "I love Questco and I'd do anything for this place," I knew a resignation was imminent. That's a confusing message for a new leader to hear. The wave of departures created a major challenge, especially when the entire team in one department left and most of the managers of another important group departed. In the upcoming chapters, I'll discuss how I set about rebuilding trust in the company leadership. Although the challenges I faced may be quite different from yours, morale and retention are universal issues in all organizations.

A LITTLE MORE ABOUT ME

That first morning at Questco, I toured the building and tried to shake every employee's hand, realizing that we were all a bit trepidatious about the future. I felt blessed for being given the opportunity that the job afforded me. But I had a lot to contemplate during my drive home, ninety minutes in Friday evening traffic. I had some comfort that I had made a good impression because the board chairman and another board member, who had planned to stay all day, left by midmorning after expressing satisfaction with our handling of the transition. I had done something else too. I had hit reset on my professional life, and not for the first time.

I had spent the previous four years in an extremely hard-charging workplace in several executive roles for Insperity's boutique middle market division. That period was my only experience working in the HR outsourcing industry, because I have a résumé that nobody would ever build by design. My undergraduate degree in accounting was a practical decision—looking for a safe and well-paying job in an adverse economy. By age nineteen I was an intern at Deloitte, wearing an ill-fitting $100 suit but getting to hobnob with real businesspeople. I thought that was pretty cool, so I became a CPA, auditing financial statements. I loved everything about being at an international accounting firm except the actual audit work, which I found to be a poor fit for someone who is improvisational and entrepreneurial and has broad interests.

My lifelong friend Michael Berger and I decided to become franchisees with a direct-mail marketing company, Money Mailer. Starting a small business and watching it grow was rewarding in a visceral way. Our Money Mailer clients were themselves small businesses, which make a difference in people's lives and are important to their communities and our society. One particular client we were marketing in our mailings, Pizza Chef, caught our attention. We gave up our direct-mail business and agreed to open the sixth gourmet pizza restaurant in a fast-growing franchise operation. I stayed in that business for only four years, but I can still throw a pretty decent pizza crust.

Feeling underprepared for the demands of entrepreneurship, I returned to school full time to complete my MBA at Northwestern University's Kellogg School of Management. I then plunged into the corporate world at Goldman Sachs and Boston Consulting Group before eventually becoming the director of brand marketing for Maritz, a storied B2B company. Maritz is a 125-year-old, billion-dollar marketing services company that provides performance improvement, group and incentive travel, and consumer insight services to large global organizations. From there, I joined my brother's e-commerce company that I described in the book's introduction.

It was as the CEO of that fast-growing online ticket selling company that I was introduced to the support of a PEO, as a client of Insperity. This overwhelmingly positive experience led me to be an evangelist for Insperity and for outsourced HR more generally. After our organization was sold to a strategic buyer, I had the opportunity to consult for a wide variety of organizations on issues ranging from brand communication to finance to transportation logistics. Through this diversity of experience, I would often find myself reflecting on how powerful outsourced HR was as a value driver. I followed the industry, invested in shares of the publicly held companies, and recommended outsourced HR to anyone who would listen. When my friends at Insperity reached out with a newly created role to accelerate growth in their middle market practice, I jumped at the opportunity. And I spent nearly four years communicating and sharing the value of outsourced HR with strong support from the people who pioneered the industry.

When I became CEO of Questco, in some ways I had been preparing for the job my entire life and was very ready for it. But there's another way in which an executive can never really be prepared for such a position. A CEO never knows what is around the corner because we are dealing with the fascinating, complicated, and messy behavior of human beings. Certainly, I have learned a lot of helpful things on the job since my "coronation" as CEO, and I will be learning more alongside you as I discuss my ideas and get feedback from readers. I think my experience, like my résumé, is unique on the surface, but underneath, it shares the common phenomena faced by organizational leaders. We can all feel competent, confident, scared, and overwhelmed at the same time, even though those conflicting feelings frequently go unacknowledged. My goal in this book is to help make leaders more effective by showing them that they are not alone in those feelings.

MY INSIDE-OUT NARRATIVE

I started off telling you about myself and my company because I have organized the book as an inside-out narrative. We begin with how leaders have to care for themselves, then we zoom out to see how leaders care for their teams. And finally, we explore what leaders can do to care for their clients or customers.

Chapter 2 will suggest that the real culprit behind CEO anxiety is the myth of executive exceptionalism and that buying into the CEO superhero myth internalizes impossible expectations at the expense of the organization. Chapter 3 will demonstrate how much more leaders will achieve—and how much better they'll feel—when they begin treasuring their support system. That idea will be further developed in chapter 4: leaders who understand the power of their team serve that team, creating a feedback loop whereby the teams support the leaders. The underlying concept of servant leadership may be familiar to you, but to apply it—which can be as simple as just acting like a human being—it helps to see the idea in action. I hope my candid stories and the people I introduce in chapter 5 will bring home the power of the concept.

Moving on to how leaders pursue external goals, chapter 6 offers insight into how to clarify an organization's purpose in order to better serve clients. This chapter discusses the limits of our power and control and how to set actionable goals using best-selling author Shawn Achor's circles of influence. Chapter 7 starts by acknowledging that no plan survives contact with reality and explores how corporate leaders can take an improvisational approach in dealing with chaos, crises, and volatility. Finally, chapter 8 reviews the book's key insights and suggests some next steps.

In this chapter, I shared what I was thinking, feeling, and doing as I took on a new challenge as a CEO. The point was to show how I had to convey confidence and optimism despite my fears and uncertainties. If you are in any kind of situation in which you don't have all the answers or don't even know what questions you are facing, you see that you are not alone. Maybe you are not a CEO yet, but your current position or a recent promotion has thrust new leadership demands on you. Maybe you have made it into the corner office suite because you have extraordinary talents and great ideas, or maybe you were just born into the right family. Whatever your circumstances, expectations may seem impossible at times. The next chapter, which addresses the CEO superhero myth, will tell you how to thrive during those times when you feel overwhelmed or outmatched.

CHAPTER TWO

AVOIDING THE CEO SUPERHERO TRAP

W hen we as business leaders feel overwhelmed, the reason is that we sense a gap between what's expected of us and what we're capable of, and most of the time we're right. We may be in the corner office, but the possibility of failure is lurking around every turn.

It's fundamentally unfair that we're in this position where we—and seemingly everybody around us—believe it's *all* up to us. We think that one great leader will drive the success of the enterprise, that one person will set the goals and chart the course to reach them. What's really being set up is an impossible expectation for those assuming a senior leadership role. We feel underprepared, because logically we can't do everything, no matter how rich or diverse a background we amassed as we worked our way up to the top. We can't know everything about finance, operations, products, marketing, and building a team. All these areas are necessary for business success. As we'll see in this chapter, thinking that we need to do it all alone is an attitude that undermines our best efforts and feeds our worst anxieties.

ORIGINS OF THE HERO MYTH

The myth of the superhero CEO is deeply rooted in our culture. Think back to your ninth-grade history class, where you learned about the rugged individualism that defined the United States and our Manifest Destiny. These notions echo in the contemporary media coverage of business executives. On the covers of business magazines, we see proud men or women, arms folded, promising to tell their story of how they alone were leading their enterprise to conquer new frontiers of success or how they alone could save it from oblivion. Even if the enterprise has tens of thousands of employees, popular culture tells us that one exceptional CEO must have had the vision: Apple would be nothing without Steve Jobs. Jeff Bezos made Amazon a trillion-dollar company in less than twenty-five years. Mark Zuckerberg created Facebook, and he alone will determine its fate. From Lee Iacocca at Chrysler back in the day to Elon Musk at Tesla, we're thinking of one person in the corporate driver's seat.

The corollary to CEO exceptionalism is expressed in the adage "Fake it till you make it." Inevitably, times will come when we feel like we can't possibly measure up to the exceptional standard. Anxiety creeps in, and along with it comes isolation. "It's lonely at the top," the saying goes. Isolation compounds the feeling of being over-whelmed. And so what happens? We feel like a fraud or an imposter.

HUMILITY TO THE RESCUE

The best business leaders boost or restore their confidence by exercising another trait, which is humility. Humility is an essential part of confidence. How is that so? Humility allows us to feel that we don't need to know everything, do everything, be everything, in order to be successful. In fact, making impossible superhero goals is what sets people up for imposter syndrome, the uncomfortable phenomenon in which competent people doubt their accomplishments. Clinging to the concept of CEO exception-alism, feeling the need to know everything, is not only counterpro-ductive to business success but also to our happiness and well-being. Humility is the powerful link that liberates business leaders from the myth of the CEO superhero.

> **Humility allows us to feel that we don't need to know everything, do everything, be everything, in order to be successful.**

When an executive has just been promoted to lead a department, or a new CEO takes over an organization, there is often extra pressure to be a hero. Perhaps a gap in leadership must be remedied or there is a mandate to transform the organization. Change is supposed to be forthcoming, and the clock is ticking. Nobody is appointed to a job with the expectation of taking years or decades to bring about transformative change. The time pressure can deepen anxiety and feelings of being overwhelmed. If you are thinking, "I don't have the team I need to get this done, and I don't have enough time left," the situation may seem hopeless.

How is humility going to rescue the leader from such a depressing situation? Humility promotes authenticity. Let me explain by telling a cautionary story. I have seen a lot of leaders in action during years of consulting work. At one large business services organization, a new CEO came in and announced his vision for changing the company culture very clearly. His mantra was this: "First, take good care of each other." He had this message etched prominently in several places around the corporate campus, literally written in gold in two-foot-high letters. But there was a competing message in smaller type. Dominating the company's internal communications were pictures, stories, and emails about all the great places the CEO was traveling to. The self-aggrandizement turned off executives and managers who might have helped the CEO lead the cultural transformation. It canceled out the message of looking out for each other. The organization lost a lot of talent as a feeling spread through the company that the new management was more in it for themselves than for everyone else.

We'll have explanations and examples later in this book of the ways that humility and authenticity help a CEO achieve corporate goals.

TRY THIS:
A VISUAL REMINDER

A senior leader's office walls and desk often display awards and gifts. If a visitor noticed that she had a framed Wonder Woman comic book cover or emblem or that he had a Hercules action figure, it would seem like a sentimental keepsake. But it could serve as a visual reminder to avoid the hero myth described in this chapter.

My thoughts about this leadership issue formed during the years that I worked as a consultant and saw executives buying into a false narrative about their role. It was not until I began the preparation for this book that I discovered that scholars and journalists had given this phenomenon a variety of names over the years while writing about the overblown or dashed expectations surrounding "iconic" and "superhuman" CEOs or corporate "saviors." I settled on "superhero myth" as a simple but memorable term.

WHAT IF IT REALLY IS ALL UP TO YOU?

The leadership lessons we are discussing apply as much to modest firms as to corporate behemoths. About six million businesses in the United States have at least one employee but fewer than five hundred. Running one of these small businesses often can feel overwhelming, especially when resources are lacking—when there's not enough money to hire the right support team. Early in my career, I owned one of these undercapitalized small businesses, and the experience has shaped my thinking about leadership.

At the gourmet pizza restaurant that I mentioned in the previous chapter, my partner and I were so hands-on that we were covered in dough and sauce all the time. We had big dreams to expand our franchise holding into a large number of restaurants in the Saint Louis area. But at the beginning, we were running one undercapitalized restaurant with staff earning minimum wage or not much more. One particular Sunday night, we scheduled six people to work, but I was the only one who showed up to handle a busy dinner shift. It really was all up to me because I had failed to build a dependable team.

I was one of those small business owners who said things like "Nobody will care about my business as much as I do, so I have to do everything. I have to be everything." That night I ended up being the baker, the waiter, the busboy, and more. I had fallen into the trap of being the superhero instead of being a team builder. I had a newborn at home and was physically exhausted, throwing pizza crusts during the lunch rush, then trying to focus on marketing and payroll before preparing for the dinner crowd. Soon it was 1:30 a.m., and I wasn't close to being done with work. It was a victory just to live through the day, but the insanity was enough to make me realize that my business skills needed work. That's how I got motivated to go back to school and get an MBA.

COLLEGE TEAMS WITHOUT UNIFORMS

When I left the pizza business after a few years to attend Northwestern University's Kellogg School of Management, I learned through case studies how other entrepreneurs made similar mistakes of not investing enough in their support staff and trying to micromanage too many aspects of their business. (Case studies in business school are situations that academics have created to blend multiple concepts together and simulate for the students a real-life challenge that managers face.)

I remember doing a case study based on the book by Jim Collins and Jerry I. Porras, *Built to Last: Successful Habits of Visionary Companies*.[1] The authors studied eighteen long-lasting and admired companies from diverse industries. The companies prospered for generations not because of a visionary leader but because of the char-

---

1   Jim Collins and Jerry I. Porras, *Built to Last: Successful Habits of Visionary Companies* (New York: HarperBusiness, 1994).

acteristics imbued over time. That's not to deny the importance of the role of the CEO. But there is a difference between a senior leader being responsible for a lot of very important things and thinking that everything is the responsibility of that person.

To use a contemporary example, the cofounder of Apple, Steve Jobs, was famous for micromanaging product design, but I doubt he was personally involved in corporate decisions about transportation, plant security, or many other management concerns. Apple was built to last because tens of thousands of people are organized around a mission and are using their unique talents to help an enterprise succeed.

When we tackled case studies at the Kellogg School, we did it as a team, dividing up responsibilities. None of us had the benefit of job title or power within the group; all of us were dependent on our shared energies and talents to be successful. Kellogg's teamwork approach helped reinforce the lesson from the pizza parlor that in any size enterprise, work gets accomplished better in an environment where labor is divided among people who maintain supportive relationships and are willing to rely on each other. It hit home when we were assigned a famously complicated case study involving optimizing production for a national cranberry cooperative. I didn't have the background in the manufacturing industry to handle some of the heavy calculations involved—truck wait times, the mass of wet versus dry berries, and so on. Our team members were practically strangers, but everybody pulled their weight. Tapping our variety of experiences and disciplines and working together was the only way we could have gotten the project completed on time. The lesson stuck with me—most of the time.

THE LURE OF THE TOP-DOWN APPROACH

Several years after I finished business school, I was leading marketing functions for a sales services firm when my brother asked me to take over his e-commerce company. At that company, there was no way I could have made the mistake of trying to do everything myself. As I mentioned in the introduction to this book, Coast to Coast Tickets sold event tickets online, an industry and technology I knew nothing about. I didn't know how the pricing worked or who the players were, but I had a good understanding of where we wanted to get financially and culturally. I felt sure that the key to my success would be a strong vision: I would leverage my big ideas and my big ambitions to propel this team toward success.

The business was already profitable and growing but needed more organization to scale up. Tasks were not divided properly, and everybody was doing everything, a common situation with small businesses. My brother, to his credit, had the humility and confidence to acknowledge that he didn't have all the answers. He brought me in to professionalize the business, to figure out what we needed to do to grow aggressively in the right areas.

I determined that we would need to deepen our technological sophistication in order to stay efficient and that we would need to more forcefully expand into adjacent lines of business in order to broaden our reach. I took a top-down approach to pursuing that vision. I didn't formulate goals based on what my team members were seeing in the field. I didn't take the time to build consensus. I simply set the agenda, with buy-in only from my business partner brother, and I issued the orders.

As a consequence, I didn't have a good handle on how my team was reacting to the change of strategy. By the time I realized that there was dissent, it was too late to work on building consensus. Slowly, it emerged that our head of technology was subtly undermining the new initiative. This guy was a talented coder in his midtwenties with no prior management experience. Eventually, we had a confrontation over the need to get his team on board. I said, "We need you to do this." And he said, "What happens if I don't?"

That kind of defiance is not acceptable in middle management, but it also revealed that the senior leadership had not done as good a job as we should have of establishing the company culture. We could not have a department leader willing to implement only the decisions that he agreed with. He had to leave the company quickly and be replaced with someone culturally aligned with what we were trying to accomplish. Avoiding the trap of the CEO superhero myth involves not just realizing that you can't do everything yourself and delegating authority. You also must bring on people who can be an extension of your vision, who buy into it fundamentally.

A MENTALLY HEALTHY APPROACH

The entrepreneurial spirit that makes some people believe they can create or lead a business turns out to have a dark side. Research shows that small business owners have more emotional issues, such as depression, than the US population as a whole. For example, Dr. Michael A. Freeman of the University of California, San Francisco led a 2015 study asking entrepreneurs and a demographically matched comparison group about their mental health.[2] About half of the entrepreneurs self-reported having one

---

2   Michael A. Freeman, "Are Entrepreneurs Touched with Fire?," updated April 15, 2015, https://michaelafreemanmd.com/Research_files/Are%20Entrepreneurs%20Touched%20with%20Fire%20(pre-pub%20n)%204-17-15.pdf.

or more lifetime mental health conditions, as opposed to about a third of the comparison group. The entrepreneurs were significantly more likely to report a lifetime history of depression, ADHD, substance use conditions, and bipolar diagnosis.

A World Economic Forum report in 2019 examined the mental health of entrepreneurs in depth and made the following recommendations:[3]

- Destigmatizing entrepreneurs' mental health challenges through open communication and support

- Investors setting aside some of their financial support to be used for company founders' personal well-being

- Including mental health professionals in the organizational support systems

Concern for the psychological well-being of business leaders extends beyond the familiar emotions of feeling lonely at the top and anxious about their abilities and prospects for success. Our economy relies on entrepreneurs, and our businesses need entrepreneurial leaders, so it is important to understand and address their vulnerabilities.

THE SENIOR LEADER'S DOMAIN

Accepting that the senior leader can't be everywhere and do everything raises the question, "What is the role's mandate?" The senior

---

3   Marcel Muenster and Paul Hokemeyer, "There Is a Mental Health Crisis in Entrepreneurship. Here's How to Tackle It," World Economic Forum, March 22, 2019, https://www.weforum.org/agenda/2019/03/how-to-tackle-the-mental-health-crisis-in-entrepreneurship.

leader's job, in the simplest terms, is to define what success looks like and the timeline to get there. But that mandate comes with a disclaimer: just because this is your responsibility doesn't mean that you accomplish it alone. Whether it is setting financial goals or building a company culture, the senior leader may or may not have the background and expertise to proceed solo on any given task. Relying on the right people is the best way to get optimal results. It's also crucial to recognize outside factors that control the timeline. For example, in my current position, the factors I take into consideration regarding our company's timeline and financial goals are not only our internal capabilities but also the commitments made by our private equity ownership to its investors.

Defining success and timeline is no simple task, and I don't want to minimize the work, talent, and perseverance necessary to be a senior leader. Figuring out an attainable goal is one challenge. Another is making sure that the company builds and maintains the necessary attributes to get there. The leader must not only define the end point but also articulate and constantly evangelize the vision, with authenticity. Although they can delegate many tasks and decisions, the senior-most leaders must be the standard bearers for the company culture, every day and with every action. They must understand and articulate what key performance indicators mark the company's progress along its timeline and establish accountability in the management ranks. To keep everyone on track, they must listen, observe, experiment, and make course corrections.

> **The leader must not only define the end point but also articulate and constantly evangelize the vision, with authenticity.**

Confidence and humility are the personal attributes necessary for long-term success in this domain. These attributes allow a leader to build and rely on a strong team and to trust others to work independently, in coordination with each other, and in sync with the timeline. Confidence allows leaders to inspire team members who must be depended on for success. Humility keeps leaders from overestimating their own abilities.

TRY THIS:
COMPLETELY LET GO OF SOMETHING

Relying on the team takes practice. If you are one of those leaders whose personality makes it difficult for you to give up control, start with something small. Select a task that has a limited downside if things go wrong. It can involve planning an internal meeting or even a company social event, but it must be something that legitimately needs to be done, not make-work. Place this task completely in the hands of team members who may have the ability to step up and do it well. Then stay away completely, allowing them to both struggle and succeed independently. If they do a great or even a satisfactory job, you will be building shared confidence in their ability to take on fuller responsibility for tasks with greater strategic or financial consequence. In the unlikely event that they fail in the task, it will still be a learning experience. We'll have more to say in chapters 4 and 5 about addressing failures in a straightforward way without anger.

RECOGNIZING THE CEO SUPERHERO MYTH AT WORK

One of my consulting engagements exposed me to a niche industry corporation whose founder and CEO very much bought into the superhero myth. He profoundly believed that whenever he wasn't personally involved, things would get screwed up. His company had risen to a level of prominence and success that allowed it to attract pretty good talent. But those recruits soon began to feel micromanaged and undermined. In an organization that could have only one genius deciding everything from the top, they felt that their talent was wasted and that they were not making a difference. They moved on to another organization where they could show their own genius by making brilliant decisions. The inability to retain talent detracted from the success of the enterprise.

At a nationwide marketing agency that I once worked with, the CEO liked to show up at every client pitch and would sometimes interject remarks that undermined the team that worked on the presentation. They either had to change their presentation on the fly or just let their work product and their reputations be marginalized. The employees felt disenfranchised, helpless, and detached. If the boss was going to come in and change things on a whim, why bother to do anything special? A leader who engages in such pernicious behavior will be left with a bunch of yes-people in a company that ultimately underperforms. That result creates a vicious cycle in which the underperformance appears to confirm the belief that the leader *does* need to do it all. The superhero myth becomes self-fulfilling.

The cycle generally runs like this: it starts with a fundamental belief, whether throughout the organization or at the top, that the superhero leader must do all and be all. This belief leads to learned helplessness from others. (When Superman was watching over Metropolis, who felt they should step up and fight alongside him?) Decision-making, risk-taking, independent thought, and initiative wither. People who feel that they are just extras in the superhero saga grow less accountable. People who hunger for accomplishments and want to contribute toward shared goals go elsewhere, leaving only those who perform to minimum expectations. Because the remaining team is not able or interested in independent initiative, it falls to the superhero to do everything and to make every decision of consequence.

Fortunately, the cycle can be broken using techniques we'll discuss in the rest of this book. The first step is for senior leaders to realize that they can't do it all themselves. Once they understand the superhero myth, they can overcome it. As the examples in this chapter have shown, the phenomenon affects businesses of all sizes, from one with marble pillars on its corporate campus to a neighborhood pizza restaurant owned by two guys in their twenties.

LEARNING FROM EXPERIENCE

This concludes the doom-and-gloom section of the book. I started the chapter by warning you that failure was lurking around every corner and that any of us could get fired at any time. I suggested that your dream-job promotion would make you feel anxious, incompetent, lonely, and depressed. I recounted my meltdown in my pizza restaurant in the middle of the night that led to my going back to business school. Earning an MBA taught me how to do case studies, but I had to learn more about people management through experience. This included an unpleasant confrontation resulting from top-down change management and being exposed as a consultant to senior leaders whose hubris undermined their companies.

Human beings are complicated, fascinating, and unpredictable, which makes people management a skill that executives must continually learn on the job. I discussed two traits, confidence and humility, that help senior leaders establish a culture that aligns their people with the end point they want to reach and the timeline for getting there.

In the next chapter, we look at *how* to establish that company culture in which engaged, happy, and productive employees help their company succeed.

CHAPTER THREE

TREASURE YOUR SUPPORT SYSTEM

The day I started as CEO at Questco, you may recall from chapter 1, I spoke of four key attributes to the company culture that I sought to develop: simplicity, authenticity, electricity, and accountability. Now let me introduce you to four people who embody these attributes, because it is the inspirational people whom I have met throughout my career who have shaped my thinking about company culture. Once you meet these people, you'll better understand how a senior leader can avoid the trap of the CEO superhero myth by building an enviable support system.

SIMPLICITY

When I think about the concept of simplicity in terms of communication, thought, and purpose, Kathy Johnson comes to mind. Kathy is a no-BS straight shooter whose South Jersey accent fits in surprisingly well in South Texas. Simple and direct, Kathy calls it like she sees it so that her team members know where they stand, and she has an uncanny ability to deliver even the harshest of messages with equal parts humanity and candor. Kathy was head of the middle market division of the multibillion-dollar, national HR services provider Insperity when I worked there. Like the other three people I will introduce you to in this chapter, she earned steady promotions to significantly greater levels of responsibility. In Kathy's case, she went from managing the middle market services group to leading the entire division, with an expanded scope into the less familiar world of sales. Any senior leaders reading this book probably have had a similar experience of suddenly being in charge of something new and having to take a much broader view of what their organization does. This expanded scope of responsibility is the point at which it becomes tempting to "fake it till you make it." But Kathy's more genuine and direct approach demonstrates one of the keys to the more successful strategy that we are forming here to "fly it while you build it."

What Kathy said to employees in her polished initial presentations conveyed a simple message: "It all starts with trust. And that starts with me—I'm going to extend trust to you first." Extending trust is a powerful way for a new leader to cut through the tension that occurs when both the boss and the employees are worrying about immediately proving themselves. Just saying that the trust was already there started things off with positive intent, but Kathy followed up by taking the time to truly understand each of our talents and our needs as individuals. Because the bedrock of our relationship was a simple concept of trust, the heavy lifting we needed to do became easier for each of us to manage. Trust enabled candid discussion, openness to varying points of view, taking appropriate risks, and acknowledging our mistakes and building something better from them. We were able to work through complex situations quickly, with Kathy's leadership giving us the freedom to get to the point faster. By coming in with a simple statement of trust and ensuring that people felt safe to be themselves, Kathy could more quickly build an enduring vision and a plan to get there. Getting people to feel comfortable supporting us as we start to build something together can be that simple.

AUTHENTICITY

My friend and colleague at Insperity, Keith Simmons, received a major promotion into senior sales leadership and found himself in a much more complicated role. A barrel-chested, born and bred Houstonian (Go Coogs!), Keith epitomizes a good ol' boy with a heart as big as Texas, a guy who's not always comfortable acknowledging that his IQ is likely north of 140. Being equal parts humble, personable, and brilliant, he brought to this role the various traits and behaviors that epitomize authenticity. Fundamentally, he was able to be himself while extending kindness to others, showing a genuine interest in people, and getting to know them. This in turn continues to inspire his team to display both fierce loyalty and exceptional performance. Authenticity is what allows a senior leader to ask a lot of questions without seeming threatening or invasive, which quickly builds affinity. When I internalized Keith's approach, I found that I saved a lot of time developing good working relationships.

ELECTRICITY

The most influential person early in my career was Matt Harris, my boss at Maritz, the giant marketing services company. I was hired into a fledgling executive rotation program, and I obtained a more solid footing within the company only when Matt recruited me into the brand communications division about nine months later. Maritz traces its history to 1894, and in a company so established, the work environment can be old school and change averse. But Matt came into his job from a much smaller firm and brought with him was a constant sense of excitement. Matt has one of the most curious, interesting minds I've known, with an appreciation for playfulness and its place in creative problem-solving. We felt that we were building something special.

A company culture with electricity not only seems to shimmer with brilliance and move at the speed of light but also sparks energy and innovation among its team members. Matt epitomizes this concept of electricity because he is brilliant intellectually and gregarious in personality in a way that allowed him to imbue his team with a sense that we were a part of something larger than ourselves. While feeling that there were great things to be done, we could give each other the opportunity to fail and to make mistakes along the way. When work has meaning, purpose, and excitement, people are more likely to give their all.

ACCOUNTABILITY

Accountability is a familiar concept in business and yet somehow elusive at many organizations. Goals come and go in an organization where the reporting lines are muddled or where plans and promises are made and then soon forgotten. At Questco, I was fortunate to be able to hire Brandon Hartsaw as chief operating officer. Brandon has the charm of a southern gentleman, which immediately puts people at ease. Drawing on an early career experience as a youth pastor, Brandon has a therapist's approach for getting people to share information candidly and completely. As a result, Brandon elicits feedback and progress reports from his team in minutes that other leaders might need hours to glean.

Brandon is a person who from a very early age was forced to grow up fast, giving him an exceptional emotional intelligence. Combining his fundamental understanding of people with his very organized way of thinking through business problems, Brandon added a structure to our organization and set standards that greatly enhanced accountability. Although he reports to me, I have learned much from him.

EMOTIONAL INTELLIGENCE

Emotional intelligence, also known as EQ, is a concept popularized by best-selling author Daniel Goleman. He identified five components that I describe briefly here because they all help senior leaders build a team and maintain a support system:

- Self-awareness—The ability to recognize and understand one's own moods and emotions and their effect on others.

- Self-regulation—The ability to control or redirect disruptive impulses and moods, and the propensity to suspend judgment and to think before acting.

- Internal motivation—A passion for work beyond money and status, pursuing goals with energy and persistence.

- Empathy—The ability to understand others' emotions and react accordingly.

- Social skills—Proficiency in managing relationships and building networks, finding common ground and building rapport.

APPLYING THE FOUR ATTRIBUTES

Having these four people in my life whose leadership attributes made such an impression on me has been a blessing during my time at Questco. I came into the CEO job with my own skill set and my own approach, but I have been inspired by the lessons I learned from Kathy, Keith, Matt, and Brandon. I hope that I can pay the debt forward by inspiring my readers with some insights into how I applied these lessons at a company that had some relatively common business challenges, such as staying relevant and competitive in a quickly changing market.

Questco was about thirty years old, and its growth had stalled. Its well-meaning, client-focused teams worked well serving the HR outsourcing needs of businesses that valued human interaction, accuracy, and our folks' pleasant attitude and willingness to fix any mistakes that might happen. In other words, we could serve a subset of clients who were not too demanding. But as the HR outsourcing industry matures, clients grow more demanding in every way. They want specialized insights, industry certifications, expertise in technology, and more. We had to broaden our appeal.

The value proposition of a company like Questco is based on a recognition that it's really challenging to operate small businesses.

They never have the money, time, and energy required to handle all the needs of their people, so it is smart to reach out for help with HR. For the clients to trust us to take good care of them, we must have a healthy, supportive culture internally. Our fundamental mission is to provide the clients with a great support system, but I realized as a new leader that we had not built such a support system for ourselves. Doing so would require more than the routine CEO outreach techniques of getting to know employees in small-group meetings, having an open door, and taking a listening tour.

Managing by walking around has its merits, but my plan was less pedestrian. I needed to get to *really* know Questco's people. I had to spend enough time in one-on-one conversations or small groups to uncover their motivations, preconceived notions, attitudes, and expectations. Even deeper, I wanted to understand their family and personal dynamics, how they got to their current jobs, and their aspirations.

Such information always proves valuable to a leader, but it was especially important at the time at Questco because the company's people had been through a lot of change and some wanted to be done with it. That disaffection was something I needed to know about. Understanding people's motivations was also important to my plan of overhauling performance bonuses, which had not been handled systematically in the past. People were getting hundreds of dollars in bonus pay here and there, but it was not clear how the bonuses were promoting accountability.

With my CFO, we put a lot of work into a new incentive plan that would involve a meaningful amount of money, much more than in the past. This was a chance to show off the four key attributes: communicating the plan with simplicity and authenticity, promoting accountability, and generating electricity. Instead, there was a short circuit.

After announcing with great fanfare that people could be earning a lot more money, I was absolutely shocked that the reaction was neutral at best and profoundly negative in some individual cases. Eventually, I learned the reasons. Some people had been lured to Questco in recent years with promises—neither in writing nor realistic—that they would be getting big raises that dwarfed my promised incentive plan. The lesson I learned was that a leader inheriting a new situation must spend time understanding their people's preconceived notions and expectations. Don't expect these to be highlighted in yellow in a file memo marked with a sticky red arrow flag.

> **After announcing with great fanfare that people could be earning a lot more money, I was absolutely shocked that the reaction was neutral at best.**

TRY THIS:
TRANSFORM A CLICHÉ INTO ACTION

When a company executive says, "Our most valuable asset is our people," it sounds trite these days. A more resonant message is that how we understand and treat our people influences the *incremental effort* that they will devote to the success of the company. Nowhere is the impact of human beings more profound than in a service business where the daily interactions drive our success. But every business relies on its people. Do something every day to show that you understand that concept. It can be as simple and old school as writing a thank-you note, or you can invent your own creative way of recognizing the humanity around you.

REALLY GETTING TO KNOW PEOPLE

When I first got to know people in the usual introductory meetings, I applied what I had learned from Kathy Johnson and extended trust. But employees who already felt betrayed or at least let down because the company had not met their expectations could not return that trust and tell me everything I needed to know. Whether their expectations were realistic or not, and although the unmet promises predated my arrival, I needed to know what was weighing on the minds of my people.

Knowing the mechanics of who reports to whom is important, but so is really understanding the personal dynamics. Superficial conversation doesn't surface those undercurrents. Having an open-door policy may invite more personal conversations, but the open door doesn't ensure that people have an open heart. Here's where simplicity and authenticity come in: people who don't know one another well can easily speak past each other. Even if they are trying to be candid and honest, they may lack a common vocabulary. Keeping it simple—delivering a clear, concise message—helps ensure that words are taken as they are meant.

In trying to overcome the misunderstandings I encountered, I spoke transparently and openly about how the business was doing and what we could expect from each other. I tried to use language that was simple and clear enough to establish my authenticity as a straight shooter. I told people that I wanted them to speak their minds in an atmosphere of trust, without fear of reprisal. This did not happen all at once. It took a series of conversations, and notably, people in some parts of the company were more likely to feel comfortable speaking their minds. As a CEO, it can be frustrating to feel that information you need is out there but is not being shared. Imagine walking past a gaggle of smokers outdoors or a crowd gathered in a break room, and suddenly they grow quiet. What were they saying that you probably should know about?

FROM TRUST COMES INNOVATION

Remember from the last chapter the defiant technology chief we had to let go from the online ticket sales company? His successor turned out to be a highly engaged person who knew that he had our trust, and he proposed an idea that was ahead of its time. Our operation, like a lot of small, round-the-clock companies, had a challenge maintaining its servers off-site. His then-new idea was to use cloud server technology to save us the inefficiency of sending our technicians by truck to a server colocation center to figure out what was happening if our website crashed or slowed down. In that era, cloud technology was exotic and not something I grasped. But because of our mutual trust, we got on board early, resulting in dramatically better reliability and profitability.

CULTIVATING BUY-IN

A company culture does not grow and blossom uniformly, and it can wither in the shadows created by the wrong managers. Building a support system as a senior leader involves choosing other leaders who have earned your trust. For me, this would mean having direct reports and department heads who shared my beliefs about the value of the four key attributes. These managers would really understand the end point we were trying to reach, which was being able to compete with the large public companies in our industry. They would cultivate employee buy-in not only to the production and earning goals involved in getting to the end point but also to the cultural standard.

We took a sober look at different departments and how they were functioning. Where we found gaps in talent, outlook, or perspective, we needed to hire aggressively. A key hire, in addition to Brandon, was Derek Carlstrom, who would lead our sales department. He came from one of the dominant national players in our industry and brought an uplifting optimism about Questco and the sales process. In any industry, running sales is a very challenging role. Salespeople must deal with a lot of rejection and tremendous pressure to hit their numbers. You can't have a hangdog leader in sales. Derek's optimism helped his team members believe in themselves, and he continues to attract more people with similar attitudes.

Tragically, one of Derek's employees unexpectedly lost her husband, who suffered a stroke and died much too young. While the woman was out dealing with the tragedy, Derek rallied the other salespeople to cover her accounts and to make sure that her deals got done and her compensation was maintained. Everybody's selfless extra work helped Questco's bottom line of course, but the cultural impact was just as important. In some companies, salespeople have a reputation for being lone wolves concerned only with their own commissions. Questco's culture was clearly different. The entire sales organization showed up at the husband's funeral. The company not only sent flowers but also took care of meals. The employee returned to work and within six months had the largest pipeline of anyone on the sales team.

As the senior leader, my role was to realize that upping the game of the sales department was not something I could do on my own. I had to find the right person—Derek—trust him, empower him, and support him through the inevitable mistakes and setbacks that confront any manager. Avoiding the trap of CEO superhero and instead finding someone who could share my vision and transfer my beliefs was a tremendously successful approach with Derek. When we were up against major competition on a sale, where six months earlier we would have lost, given up, or tried to win with a lowball price, we can now stand toe to toe. Did I just get lucky with a good hire? Yes, I was lucky to hire Derek, who became a magnet for more similarly motivated salespeople to join Questco, but such success occurs as part of a larger support system.

STRENGTHENING THE SUPPORT SYSTEM

You cannot hire culturally compatible people without first having a strong culture, a shared vision for the future communicated with simplicity and authenticity.

> **You cannot hire culturally compatible people without first having a strong culture, a shared vision for the future communicated with simplicity and authenticity.**

In hiring, we not only screen with an objective instrument for professional competence but also prioritize cultural fit in our recruiting. Leaders like Derek in sales and Brandon on the service side help spread the understanding that our clients have a hard job running their small businesses, and we need to show through our daily behavior that we're there working for those clients. Our culture is so strong that in the rare case that a new hire does not fit in, that person will stand out quickly and not be with us for long. In an environment where people genuinely support each other, there's no room for infighting and self-interest.

In a tight labor market, a supportive culture makes it easier to recruit good people. We know this because we are able to hire faster than the industry standard, and the quality of our workforce is showing through in our financial success and our customer satisfaction scores. We're far from perfect, of course. People make mistakes, and like every organization, we have some teammates who have struggled in their roles. But we are dealing with those issues in a system that embraces a fundamental belief that we need to support each other and push decision-making capability and responsibility down deeper into the organization.

In a supportive culture, leaders show gratitude and appreciation to clients and employees in tangible and intangible ways. Both are important. Getting a financial bonus for meeting goals has what we call trophy value. A bonus is not just a monetary reward because people remember *why* they were awarded something. People who feel good about the work they do want to do more and at a higher level.

I have given a lot of thought to these concepts because my first corporate leadership post was at Maritz, a company steeped in traditional motivational theory. We were told that we employed more creative talent than any company other than Disney and Hallmark. Maritz, which began as a jewelry manufacturer and wholesaler in the nineteenth century, invented the concept of the gold watch on retirement, and the company was a thought leader on talent retention. If you want to get wonkish on this subject, you can find extensive writing by psychologists on the differences between what they call extrinsic and intrinsic motivation. If you want a very basic understanding of the concept, think of the difference between those who compete because they want to win (or not lose) and those competing for the satisfaction of doing so. Now imagine how great it is to be a leader surrounded by people eager to compete for both internal and external satisfaction.

In a set of three empirical studies across different industries, researchers examined how intrinsic and extrinsic motivation affected supervisor-rated work performance, affective and continuance commitment, turnover intention, burnout, and work-family conflict.[4] They found that intrinsic motivation was associated with positive outcomes more so than extrinsic motivation. In other words, financial rewards, which come at some cost to a business, have different and sometimes less positive outcomes than people-centered actions such as inviting employees to participate in decision-making, listening to them, and giving positive feedback when they take initiative and nonjudgmental feedback when they have problems.

My experience is that leaders can motivate by authenticity, really caring about the people who work for them, listening to them, and really knowing how things are going. This kind of culture displays gratitude and appreciation indirectly but in a genuine way. I didn't come into the CEO job prepared to be a therapist, but making people feel comfortable sharing what's going on in their lives is necessary to lead an organization of human beings. People have a lot of things happening in their lives and in their heads. Understanding both is really important in order to have an engaged workforce.

SEEING THE APPROACH AT WORK

I understand that CEOs are reluctant to invest time and energy in an initiative without knowing how success will be measured objectively. How can I measure my investment in really listening to people and

---

4   Bård Kuvaas, Robert Buch, Antoinette Weibel, Anders Dysvik, and Christina G. L. Nerstad, "Do Intrinsic and Extrinsic Motivation Relate Differently to Employee Outcomes?," *Journal of Economic Psychology* 61 (2017): 244–58.

getting to know them? I can see how many boxes of Kleenex I have gone through in my office as people share what's going on in their lives—the injuries, illnesses, and deaths of colleagues and loved ones. I know how much time I spend personally showing up as often as possible at the hospital or at funerals. Being a caretaker to a team takes a personal toll on my own emotional energy. But these efforts inspire gratitude that comes through in commissioned surveys and company ratings and reviews on independent websites such as Glassdoor.com. It is important to maintain a balance and a sense of caring for self so that you as a leader can in turn be present for and helpful to others. In the pages ahead, I will document how the approach also has succeeded in business growth and in bottom-line results.

What about the possibility that hand-holding managers set themselves up to be taken advantage of? Some people will take advantage, but their self-serving behavior becomes apparent quickly and won't last amid a supportive culture. Leaders who take the time to really know their people can evaluate requests to work remotely to accommodate a child's school schedule or take time off to deal with the infirmity or death of an elderly parent. These kinds of accommodations are not cost-free to a business, but they fundamentally represent leaders' faith that their people are good people who will do the right thing. Giving people support in their times of greatest need builds trust, respect, and gratitude that pays off in future performance.

When someone's out of work because of a family emergency, and someone else volunteers to stay late to complete a mission-critical task, that is proof of a supportive culture at work. At Questco, we're processing payroll checks for tens of thousands of people at many client companies—not the kind of task that can be put off until tomorrow. We also handle clients' sensitive human resources issues. We need the right professionals to step up when the need arises, and they do so because they care about each other and about our clients.

Discretionary work is also a good measure of company culture. We see a lot of really enthusiastic volunteering to plan celebrations such as holiday parties or baby showers, time-consuming tasks that nobody has to do. This enthusiasm was on full display when we moved into our beautiful new office space. Volunteers planned an open house for employees' families, with entertainment such as balloon animals and scavenger hunts for the kids. A lot of people brought their parents or grandparents too, because they were so proud of our company and its new home.

BEYOND THE EXPECTED

The Questco benefits department has a large team responsible for handling client issues involving health insurance, such as when someone believes a carrier has wrongly denied a medical claim. The department director, Jamara Bates, became aware of a situation in which an employee of one of our clients, what we call a worksite employee, was having trouble getting a prescription filled. It was a serious, time-sensitive medical issue, and the employee was very distressed. Jamara drove across town around ten o'clock on a Sunday night to resolve the issue.

She carried two cell phones so that she could talk to different people involved with the decision while standing in front of a twenty-four-hour pharmacy counter. Eventually, she got the prescription filled and delivered it to the employee's house. She is an executive who has no responsibility to personally perform client-facing work, but she cared enough about the client and someone she had never met to give up her Sunday night.

This chapter focused on what leaders can do to build a strong culture and support system in an organization—communicating a vision with simplicity and authenticity, cultivating an environment where there is electricity and accountability among team members. Fundamental to building a support system within the organization is acceptance of the idea that the leader is not a hero who can do it all. Leaders build a team that will support themselves and their timeline for reaching the goals they have defined. But success requires the leaders to take care of the team, to help it find and maintain motivation, energy, and enthusiasm. This nurturing role in leadership is the focus of the next chapter.

CHAPTER FOUR

THE SERVANT LEADER

We govern for the benefit of the governed.

—Plato

The late professor Robert Neuschel introduced me to the concept of servant leadership when I was studying business at the Kellogg School. Professor Neuschel was a decorated army veteran who served in the Second World War and went on to a distinguished career as a senior partner at McKinsey. He had a long second career in academia. When I met the professor, he struck me as very polished, genteel, and genuine, the kind of gentleman who loved large organizations and was beloved in them. When he walked us through the concept of servant leadership, we listened.

As is obvious from the quotation that begins this chapter from the ancient Greek philosopher Plato, servant leadership is an idea that may be older than the Parthenon and with applications for leaders, whether they are elected by the people, called to a ministry, hired to run a business, or born into royalty. For centuries, the coat of arms of the Prince of Wales has borne the motto *Ich dien*, "I serve" in German. In this chapter we'll focus on the business case for leading in a manner that encourages growth and success in others. The goals are to increase the productive capacity of those in your charge. By investing in them, you instill a deeper and firmer buy-in.

Servant leadership may come naturally to some people, but others may find it counterintuitive, especially if they are more comfortable with a "kick ass and take names" command style. In the previous chapter, we discussed taking the time to *really* listen to the problems your people want to talk about. Some readers may have thought, "Fine, but I'm not going to be wasting my time listening to people complain." Now I'm going to try to persuade those readers of the value of encouraging dissent, even listening to people complain about their boss. The servant leader not only acts as a sounding board but also encourages a freedom to experiment, which means a freedom to stumble.

> **The servant leader not only acts as a sounding board but also encourages a freedom to experiment, which means a freedom to stumble.**

People tend to work up to the level of expectations that are placed on them. To encourage employees to speak up, experiment, and innovate, leaders must show confidence not only in themselves but in the whole team. This requires, as a leader, thinking beyond the immediate impulse and minimizing negative emotional reactions. In the inevitable stumbles, the servant leader finds the lesson and the opportunities for growth.

Senior leaders must support the team members' individual goals to nurture a company culture in which people understand that more is possible collectively. No matter how brilliant and talented the CEO, it's impossible for one person to come up with all the bright ideas and to figure out how to implement them. As Steve Jobs said, "It doesn't make sense to hire smart people and then tell them what to do. We hire smart people so they can tell us what to do." Relying on the team that way is the essence of servant leadership.

Those who have really bought into the concept of leading for the benefit of those who are being led show it in their daily communication. They won't say, "He works for me," but they will say, "We work together." They will refer to their "colleagues," not their "staff." The organization is not an implement or a tool for the leader. The leader provides resources and guidance to develop and nourish the capabilities of the organization.

HALLMARKS OF THE SERVANT LEADER

Servant leaders tend to display some characteristics that really make them stand out. When I was writing this section, I realized that I could list those characteristics in a way that would create an acronym to make them easier to remember: ACCEPT, which stands for availability, candor, consistency, empathy, patience, and trust.

Availability means making sure that there is adequate time in individual or small-group meetings for people to have their say, whether it involves venting frustrations, questioning, or establishing collaboration. Leaders often use business meetings solely to get information. They need those status updates for the business to function. But from a servant leadership perspective, giving time over to the employees and coaching them is really valuable to their development and to their contribution to the organization. To be a coach, you must be available and present. In too many organizations, senior leaders mostly huddle with each other behind closed doors, and if they claim to have an open-door policy, it becomes a joke. They give up the opportunity to be the resource their people need for clarity, guidance, and growth.

Candor involves giving tough messages directly. Because the servant leader is extending a lot of trust in individuals and their performance, it's necessary to address any failures and transgressions but in a straightforward way. Coaching and building performance are not possible when the leader's voice is angry or hostile.

Consistency can refer to goals, messages, and even day-to-day procedures like ensuring that meetings are not scheduled or conducted haphazardly, wasting people's time. Consistency is a particular challenge in the commotion of a growth organization. When leaders change their minds in a fast-moving situation, that's not inconsistency as long as they properly communicate the logic behind what they are doing. The plans and promises that a senior leader communicates are like a framework for the organization, and the more consistent it is, the better the response.

Empathy in its simplest sense—being aware of and sensitive to the feelings, thoughts, and experiences of others—has often been cited as a key characteristic of servant leaders. In this book I am going further to say that nobody can be a truly effective leader without understanding the humanity behind the individuals they are expecting to lead. Eliciting strong performance from a team requires understanding the individuals' personal situations, professional challenges, strengths, and weaknesses. Leadership is not about our people bending to our will, our mood, and our style. Instead, when we meet them where they are, we get dramatically better performance and they will show much more buy-in.

Patience is a virtue that is particularly valuable to senior leaders confronting a new role or major change. We discussed in chapter 2 the need to avoid the CEO superhero myth. Recognizing that you can't do everything requires giving yourself a lot of grace. Getting used to a new team or new business direction, or perhaps different or heightened expectations, requires patience. But even in the longer term, it is important to understand that we often have to balance our lofty goals and ambitions with the fact that we have fallible human beings who must come along to achieve them. The servant leader doesn't lash out over failures or disappointing results but instead asks, "How do we learn from this? How do we grow?" The patient approach recognizes that the team members are precious, and weathering the peaks and valleys will make everybody stronger.

Trust may come last in this list, but it is really the underpinning of the entire leadership approach of building a strong support team. It is essentially impossible to delegate anything without trust. Without delegation, division of labor, and allowing people to live up to their potential, performance and accomplishments will be limited. The servant leader is emotionally investing in the individual by extending trust and can say with sincerity, "You're in this role because I know you can do it, and I trust you to do your best. And you're going to knock it out of the park." That's where the greatness happens.

OBJECTIONS AND CONCERNS

Some leaders distrust their ability to read people and prefer to rely on objective tools, tests, and measurements to get to know their team's capabilities and compatibilities. They also may be uncomfortable discussing personal matters with employees. They may perceive showing empathy as an invitation to be taken advantage of. Or they may be wary of crossing a professional or legal line if they encourage talk of sensitive issues.

What happens when the servant leader listens with empathy to the challenges of an employee strained by conflicting personal and work obligations? That leader is more likely to make accommodations such as flexible work schedules. These accommodations benefit productivity, in my experience, but that's because they are born out of a human-to-human understanding of what they're dealing with. The nature of humanity in business is both an aspiration to achieve more and an acceptance of the human condition. It's not the boss trying to be everyone's best friend; it is simply appreciating the totality of the human beings and their circumstances and living with it. ACCEPT!

The book *Seven Pillars of Servant Leadership* provides practical guidance and justification for this approach.[5] The authors, Drs. James

---

5   James W. Sipe and Don M. Frick, *Seven Pillars of Servant Leadership: Practicing the Wisdom of Leading by Serving* (Mahwah, NJ: Paulist Press, 2009).

Sipe and Don Frick, compared eleven publicly traded companies most frequently cited as being servant-led[6] with companies profiled in the best-selling book by Jim Collins, *Good to Great*.[7] Looking at companies that consistently achieved superior financial performance, Collins identified one component of their success as Level 5 Leadership, "a paradoxical combination of personal humility plus professional will." In the Sipe and Frick study, servant leadership emerged as not just a component but as the *predominant* factor for financial success. Compared with an average return of 17.5 percent among the Good to Great companies, the servant-led companies delivered a 24.2 percent return.

APPLYING THE CONCEPTS

I can show you how the leadership concepts that I am espousing have worked at my company with the leaders you met in the last chapter: Derek, running sales, and Brandon, heading service-side operations. They came into their jobs as Questco was rebuilding, not an easy time for being consistent and demonstrating patience and trust. Derek was under pressure to bring in new clients as quickly as possible, and Brandon had to retain existing clients. Questco is a performance business with a long sales cycle. Losing a client is a big deal because replacements can come slowly.

When a business is struggling with problems or making difficult personnel decisions, extending trust creates a feeling that "we're all in this together." A more common atmosphere in business-to-business sales is to tell the salespeople, "Here's your number. How you

---

6   Modern Servant Leader, "Servant Leadership Companies List," accessed October 5, 2020, http://www.modernservantleader.com/featured/servant-leadership-companies-list.

7   Jim Collins, *Good to Great: Why Some Companies Make the Leap … and Others Don't* (New York: HarperCollins, 2001).

hit it is your problem." Although Derek was in a new job with a new company and running the whole sales operation for the first time, he found time to support his salespeople, being consistently available and checking in frequently to find out how he could help them succeed. By taking an interest in the total person, he has gotten outstanding results.

Brandon took on a broad portfolio of responsibility and knew he couldn't get everything done by himself. He explicitly told his direct reports that he expected them to take ownership of issues that had to be addressed in our rebuilding. The results were a much more cohesive organization, breakthrough scores in customer satisfaction surveys, and client retention rates hitting all-time highs. Brandon's team is focused and engaged. They are doing things many of them wouldn't have thought possible a year or two earlier.

The key to all this success was extending trust. I told Derek after I hired him that he would be leading in a way that was new to him, "but I believe in you and I believe you can do this. Let's help you build the team that works for you." Of course, it's not that easy. I met with him several times a week to discuss how to deal with the inevitable struggles, the disappointing hires, and the deal that should have gone our way but didn't. Eventually, the successes in sales increased, and the ethos of trust spread throughout the organization.

A CLOSE-TO-HOME INSPIRATION

I'll mention one more person who inspired my thoughts about servant leadership—my late father. He was a psychotherapist, a very empathic person, and beloved by colleagues in the large practice where he worked. He was a role model for me not because of any business acumen but because of the joy he gained from helping other people.

I learned a lot about parenting from my father's style of being present, supportive, and invested deeply in the interests of his children. He was a raving fan of whatever we were involved in. Within the family we like to tell an odd story about what happened when my sister-in-law, Alison, developed a fascination with ferrets. My father set about to learn everything he could about ferrets and became even more devoted to them than Alison. On a more serious note, we knew while growing up that whatever our pursuit was, both Mom and Dad would be fully supportive and available with unconditional love. That emotional nourishment in turn engendered quite a bit of confidence in my brother and me.

The availability, empathy, patience, and trust that were so prominent in my upbringing gave me a great grounding that I want to pay forward. I try to emulate the deep emotional support in my own parenting and business relationships. Whether it's my daughter or a young business colleague talking about some new trend I haven't caught up with, sometimes I just have to say, "Hey, I don't know what you're talking about, but if you set your mind to it, you can do it."

Sometimes at Questco I hear employees say that they feel they are among family. It's very sweet to have that genuine emotional attachment. At the same time, I know that business decisions often require emotional detachment. I tend to refer to those at work not as family but as teammates. Sometimes a coach or manager has to trade or release a player, but teammates are known for providing mutual support. The resulting atmosphere of safety can drive people to achieve much more than they thought possible.

Sometimes leaders pick up a different style of parenting in which they treat employees like children and say something like "Do it because I said so." These bosses are not persuading anyone but instead are communicating that the person receiving their orders lacks the capacity to make decisions. When there are disagreements, someone must be empowered to make a final decision if airing out the different perspectives doesn't result in a consensus. And occasionally an emergency requires quick action without discussion. But treating employees like children is a sign of failure because they will be less willing and able to step up to take adult-level responsibilities when you need them to.

COACHING VERSUS COMMANDING

Feeling a need to issue repeated "do it because I said so" commands is a sign of trouble that should prompt some introspection about why commands are necessary. If people aren't behaving in a way that gets you closer to the goal, either they don't understand or they don't agree. If a senior leader is thinking with a long enough vision and time horizon, there should be an opportunity to bring other people into the decision-making process. Getting divergent perspectives is the essential value of diversity in an organization.

> **Getting divergent perspectives is the essential value of diversity in an organization.**

Leaders who commonly resort to issuing commands are conditioning their people to not take much ownership. Employees who believe they are valued only for their labor and not for their minds won't bother to come up with fresh ideas because the boss will just tell them how it needs to be. Or they will take their fresh ideas elsewhere.

The opposite approach of coaching employees to develop executive skills is an essential part of servant leadership. Being available, giving feedback, encouraging better performance, and setting expectations is what a coach does for a team. In business, where reporting lines are more hierarchical, a servant leader CEO may coach a department head to coach line managers and so on, creating a supportive company culture.

Servant leadership is more arduous and time consuming than stepping out of the corner office and issuing commands, but the payoff is exponentially larger. Senior leaders unwilling or unable to prioritize developing and leveraging the talents of the team will be limited to what they alone know how to accomplish. They will miss out on the team's creative contributions and collective talents.

REAPING THE BENEFITS

Over my career, I have been fortunate to have had several bosses who took the time to really understand me, my needs, and my ambitions at that moment and to figure out a mutually beneficial course. Scott Bush, who was chief marketing officer at Maritz when he hired me, extended a lot of trust to let me try different things. Bush's family has produced two presidents of the United States, so you might expect him to be a hard-driving commander-in-chief, but he gave me a lot of latitude and autonomy as a relatively junior marketing executive. In particular, I recall his patience when one of our marketing campaigns debuted to a decidedly mixed response. In an attempt to appeal to the notoriously risk-averse, detail-oriented audience of meeting professionals, we depicted a series of worst-case scenarios, such as being attacked by bears or being buried alive. The hair-raising approach met with equal parts acclaim and controversy. It generated business—eventually, after long months of fear, uncertainty, and doubt—thanks to Scott's confidence and steadiness.

When I think back to my arrival at Questco, when I set out to really get to know the people on my team, there was not a clear delineation between those contributing to the company's success and those detracting from it. Everybody has strengths and weaknesses, but there was a lot on both sides of the ledger with some of our people. I could have cleaned house and replaced them, but I felt that it was my responsibility to figure out whether we could put their talents to use somehow. Maybe they were just in the wrong job. In fact, we were able to move someone from a detail- and deadline-driven role to a different job that took advantage of the person's strengths on the human side of business relationships.

That successful outcome was made possible by following the principles of servant leadership. A senior leader coming into a new situation encounters a jumble of conflicting information and feedback. Instead of making decisions that affect people's lives with very little information, the servant leader extends trust and takes the time to listen and understand the people, what they bring to the table, and what they would like to do. By asking the right questions persistently, we salvaged a career and the organization gained tremendous value.

Most organizations say, "We'll take care of you if you deliver results." The approach that has worked for me is the opposite one, which says, "We'll take care of you so that you can deliver results."

Ultimately, the leader with the heart of a servant is the one who succeeds. This leader cultivates intense loyalty and extraordinary performance. Servant leaders get results, and they make everyone's lives better in the process. In the process, they focus not only on business outcomes but also on the humanity of the team. That human aspect is the subject of the next chapter.

CHAPTER FIVE

WELCOME TO HUMANITY

We've dispensed with the myth of the CEO superhero, but that doesn't rule out the possibility that the senior business leader is a supervillain. Very early in my career, I encountered one of these corporate creeps when I took a job in New York, where I would have to fly home to see my family (including my toddler daughter) on weekends. Knowing that I had a flight to catch after work on Friday, my boss would concoct reasons why I needed to stay late. What better way for a boss to lord over the underlings and show who was in charge? The bullying, such as being grilled in front of colleagues, was almost like a fraternity pledge lineup. When I had the temerity to ask, "Hey, can I go catch my plane or not?" he answered, "That's up to you, but you're going to have to accept the consequences of leaving early." Seeing my young child was incredibly important to me, so I left. I didn't want to work in an environment where I would be forced to choose between work and family. That company is doing fine, and so am I, but in the pages ahead, we'll look at reasons why showing concern for employees' personal welfare is the right way for a business leader to behave.

Reflecting on misbehavior that all of us have seen, I can draw a few composite caricatures of villainous CEOs. Together these archetypes form a cautionary tale on the way to our goal of learning to lead like a proper human being.

Commander Brown Nose is a leader who manages up the chain with grace and skill but is a cruel taskmaster behind the scenes. The disgruntled rank and file can be mystified by the upward career momentum of such leaders. The workers don't see the side of Commander Brown Nose that is gregarious and charming in the boardroom, in the executive suites, and in dealing outside the organization with customers. The board or the bosses don't realize that the happy, accommodating person they have come to know acts just the opposite with subordinates.

I first encountered this archetype early in my career when I was still studying for the CPA exam while working as a junior auditor. The firm where I worked represented itself in its corporate branding and marketing as appreciating the importance of a good work-life balance and promoting individual achievement. An amalgam boss I'll call Tim went out of his way to make sure that my life was as painful as possible. He would schedule a meeting or demand a deliverable knowing that it would make me miss my review class. Relishing his power, he gleefully watched me struggle to organize my life around his demands. He could be arbitrary, inauthentic, distant, and unapproachable, and he could play favorites and withhold trust—all behaviors that are the opposite of the servant leadership described in the previous chapter.

Of course, such behavior is bad for business because it breeds active resentment. At its extremes, it cultivates absenteeism and even outright theft by employees who imagine they are entitled to award themselves compensatory damages. Even a minimal level of failure to care for employees in an organization's prescribed way threatens the incremental efforts of talented people who the business needs to thrive. Eventually, the ones who have choices will go elsewhere, leaving the company with a suboptimal workforce. Because the damage occurs slowly over time, and good-hearted people cover up lapses, the inauthentic behavior of a self-serving Commander Brown Nose may persist for far too long.

The Emotional Vampire is heroic at getting the job done but is a villain because of an utter lack of concern about anything other than meeting deadlines. This boss may actually tell employees, "Leave your personal life at home." The Emotional Vampire doesn't take pleasure lording over workers because that would involve seeing the team members as human beings rather than as producers of deliverables.

Drawing from my own early-career experiences, here's a fictitious example we'll call Jack and how he would deal with a rookie mistake. A junior staffer at a consulting company is learning on the job how to manipulate the millions of lines of different data that are tracked at giant consumer-goods corporations. He readily admits to Jack that he has made data-analysis errors in a draft report sent to a client. In the eyes of the Emotional Vampire, mistakes may be inevitable, but they are not forgivable. Jack doesn't acknowledge that people learn from mistakes and grow. Instead, he takes the project away and assigns the young consultant much more basic, almost clerical tasks. Transferring a project to someone more capable may be a proper decision because leaders must hold team members accountable. But humiliating rather than trying to develop the capabilities of a junior staffer is the opposite of human-centered leadership.

This approach—all stick and no carrot—is bad for business despite its focus on productivity and output. The insidious effect is that employees are afraid to ask for guidance or own up to mistakes. In an atmosphere of fear and distrust, any mistake must be blamed on someone else, which makes the workplace more tense and hurts performance.

The Ultimate Buddy is a harder to recognize villain. The boss who wants to be a friend may seem very appealing to the team members who want to be liked and supported on the job. One consequence can be favoritism that causes resentment and divisiveness. But the biggest reason the Ultimate Buddy is bad for business is a lack of accountability among the team. An adage I have heard throughout my career is that as a manager, you get the behavior you tolerate. These Ultimate Buddy leaders will tolerate almost anything because what they want most is the approval of their team. They want to be liked rather than respected for their effectiveness. Inevitably these nice guys end up with an underperforming team, just as the harsh leaders do, because top performers prefer to go work where slackers are *not* tolerated.

Unfortunately, I need look no further than my own family for an example. When my grandfather came back home after World War II, he went into business as owner of a Standard service station in a steel mill town in southern Illinois. A gregarious, larger-than-life personality, he was everyone's friend. He was the guy who buys rounds of drinks for everyone at the bar. His generosity spilled over into his business practices, and he was quick to extend his customers credit and give his employees cash advances. When it came time to collect on the debts, he didn't have the heart to play the heavyweight role. If the employees came in late to work, goofed off on the job, or even messed up a car repair, he let it slide. Not surprisingly, the business failed because he reached a point where he couldn't pay his bills. There's nothing left of the station, unless someone is selling the iconic red, white, and blue torch sign on eBay.

HUMANITY WITH ACCOUNTABILITY

Human-centered servant leadership works only in a context in which business leaders are accountable for the results they produce. Being overly nice and ignoring business realities is just as damaging as being a monster. Human-centered leadership involves a balanced approach in which the boss is completely tuned in to the people who work in the organization and how to manage that asset to produce sustained success. Nobody is in business just to make their employees happy. The effective manager creates a structure and accountability in which people can thrive and feel supported while being held to necessary standards.

> **The effective manager creates a structure and accountability in which people can thrive and feel supported while being held to necessary standards.**

The leaders I have admired most have found ways to recognize the humanity of their people and enable them to contribute to exceptional results.

I have seen it happen at my company. Thinking back to our discussion in chapter 3 about how to cultivate a company culture, I told you about how our sales department rallied to support one of its own when she tragically lost her husband. As I write this, she is back at work and is our top business development manager as measured by revenue for the past year. She was so appreciative of the atmosphere of safety and support provided by Questco VP Derek Carlstrom and her other colleagues that her loyalty and affection for the organization strengthened her job performance. She's viewed as a leader among her peers only months after this devastating loss.

CEOs have to be accountable too. We're not immune from worrying about losing our jobs by making mistakes or failing to deliver expected results. In my case, I report to the board of directors of a private equity firm. Such firms have an image of being solely bottom-line oriented, if not rapacious monsters stripping the assets out of the companies they control. Fortunately, that stereotype does not apply to Questco's owner, Parallel49 Equity, or its chairman, Nick Peters. Nick has the training of an accountant and the heart of a therapist; he exudes both warmth and intellect as he provides helpful guidance to me as we build the business. From the moment I was hired, I was always encouraged to upgrade the business by attracting and investing in talent. Not long ago, under time pressure, I gave Nick a less than rigorously vetted proposal to present to the board. He realized that it was not going to produce a good financial outcome. He didn't scream, "What the hell is this!" or throw the papers back at me in disgust. He is a gentleman.

"You're doing a great job," Nick assured me. "A lot of things are going well, but when you do something like this, here's how I see it turning out." He walked me through why my plan wouldn't fly. I left chastened but not discouraged—and with a broader perspective. I was ready and eager to work on strengthening my plan because Nick didn't put me down; he built me up by acting like a kindly teacher trying to explain a wrong answer to a student. "I know you're better than this," he seemed to be saying. I left with the confidence that I could come back with an improved plan, and that's exactly what happened. The course correction delivered positive results for Questco. But it's easy to imagine the bad outcome that would have resulted if I were reporting to a supervillain. How successful could a company be with a CEO questioning his self-worth and afraid to advance bold proposals?

BUILDING PEOPLE UP SYSTEMATICALLY

It's good for business to have a leader with a warm personality creating a safe environment for people to experiment and use their talents. It's even better when that same leader creates a support structure, as Questco COO Brandon Hartsaw has done. He came into a thirty-year-old organization that lacked the systems and processes needed to scale up. We had to hire for his team someone expert at analyzing business processes, measuring needs and capabilities, and acquiring, creating, and implementing better systems. The young woman we hired, Mallory Glessner, did not have a long track record of managing people, and we were putting her in a tough spot. To make our processes more consistent and efficient, she inevitably would have to tell people who had been doing a job for many years that they were doing it wrong or at least could do it better.

Mallory is at a relatively early career stage for her role, but she is a Six Sigma Black Belt. (Six Sigma is a common term in business for taking a systematic, numbers-driven approach to control processes. Professional training programs based on the principles of Six Sigma offer certifications at various levels. As in the martial arts, the highest level is black belt certification.) Her job involves identifying needs that others might not see—in other words, being a set of fresh eyes. This role can easily devolve into belittling people if approached with a sense of superiority. Aided by Brandon's coaching and her own inherent concern for others, Mallory has demonstrated the humility of servant leadership and conveyed the message, "I'm here to make your work better."

Mallory's influence on training at Questco is worth discussing in some detail for this reason: it exemplifies the humility and basic human decency of servant leadership. Her statistical and analytical approach to process improvement found that certain departments were lacking necessary skill sets. Rather than calling the departments or individuals out as deficient, she used her findings to highlight the need for a training program, which she proceeded to build, implement, and *market internally* in a way that made people feel good. Individuals who might have been berated for a lack of skills by an Emotional Vampire-style leader instead felt positive about working for a company that was investing in their careers. The program we now call Questco University is still in its early stages, but it has shown success. We created it mostly to help people who had been with the company a long time catch up their skills, but we're also now better equipped to upskill new employees when necessary. That's a smarter way to do business than treating under-skilled new hires like a virus that you can't wait to get rid of.

TRY THIS:
CHAMPION PROGRAM

In implementing a change that's likely to result in some pushback, Questco Continuous Improvement Director Mallory Glessner recommends naming some early adopters as "champions" of the program. You want your people who understand and agree with the impending change to be role models. Instead of just hoping that happens, proactively identify them as the champions of the change, ready and willing to coach their teammates through any difficulties and fears. The program goes beyond the concept of training the trainers. The champions notion pushes the senior leadership's positivity about the change more deeply through the organization.

Besides addressing deficiencies in skills, our training program has helped us in two other ways: escaping the silo effect and positioning ourselves for growth. Questco historically hired many people for their specialized expertise. A payroll specialist, for example, might not know much about what our business services involve outside the silo of the payroll department. We want to teach our people to understand their job in the context of how we add value overall for clients as an outsourced HR organization. That understanding creates a more loyal, motivated, innovative, and cohesive team. We also use training to broaden skills within specialties. To continue growing, Questco must attract clients with more intensive or complicated needs. If that payroll specialist has been serving only companies with simple needs, additional training will position us to be a more sophisticated and successful organization. If the employee achieves a skills certification along the way, that's a win-win for the individual and the company and a victory for human-centered leadership.

PUTTING HUMAN LEADERSHIP TO THE TEST

Many organizations probably have shared the daunting experience of implementing a customer relationship management system for the first time. Documenting interactions in the comprehensive CRM software replaces a lot of legacy behavior—and not just at organizations mired in a bygone era of spreadsheets and Post-it notes. Implementation is not just a technical job. There are human aspects to getting people to accept the changes, to adjust their attitudes, and to see what the new technology can do for them. Looking back at the folks we met in this chapter, which one do you think will get the most return for investment on a CRM?

Commander Brown Nose will command compliance: "We're going this way, and you need to get on the bus … or get out." Then he will report that all are aboard, whether they are or not. The Emotional Vampire will issue the same command but humiliate and drive away anyone who doesn't jump aboard. The Ultimate Buddy will tolerate stragglers doing things the old way and will make lots of exceptions to accommodate objections. My money is on Mallory, who successfully marketed new CRM technology to our staff as an enhancement to help our clients, make us more effective, and make our jobs easier.

Contributing to Mallory's success were two key factors. The first was her acknowledgment that she, too, is not a superhero. She assembled a coalition of peers and volunteers from all parts of our organization—most notably fellow director Amanda Harper, who brought complementary skills and tremendous enthusiasm to move this initiative forward. Second, Mallory was thoughtful in gaining senior-level support—delivering a clear message with simplicity, as explained in chapter 3. A CEO must communicate expectations during major changes in a large organization, but frontline managers are more important in driving the message home and winning over the hearts and minds of their people. One person can be a change agent, but a cooperative effort is needed to marshal the resources and enthusiasm required for an organization to embrace major changes in systems and processes.

A human-centered leader won't be ruffled—but also won't give in—when people complain about changes or ask to be exempted from compliance. In such a situation, we might say something like, "I get it. This is a frustrating transition. Change is always hard, in the short term. But once we get through this, your job is going to be easier and you're going to be more effective." Going into some detail about the advantages generally is worth the time it takes. We can acknowledge whatever is causing frustrations: "We know it's slowing you down now, but the company really needs you to be on board with this change. Once we have the system fully implemented, everyone will benefit from the fuller picture we'll have of our sales process." The message—"Give it your best effort, and keep trying"—should be delivered early and often and by more than one person.

PROFILES IN HUMAN BEING LEADERSHIP

You have to be a commanding figure to be entrusted to run a fleet of twenty-six ships and more than forty thousand personnel. But the president of Carnival Cruise Line, Christine Duffy, is someone I think of mostly as warm and supportive. I worked with Christine when she was president of Maritz Travel and when I had various roles in the corporate office. In my last year at Maritz, my responsibility for corporate branding got me involved in something outside my area of expertise. We had decided to create an unprecedented event for the incentive industry. This type of corporate extravaganza is like a huge trade show, with sponsorship money in the seven figures, but more targeted to bring together the key people from very large corporations to hear the latest thinking in the industry from experts at Maritz and elsewhere. The speakers had to be top notch, the setting elegant, and the logistics well executed.

To do my part, I needed a lot of support from colleagues at Maritz, which fortunately has a company culture that would never allow a junior executive to flounder. I went to Christine to find out how I could get some high-profile resort and cruise line companies involved (that is, putting up big bucks). She wasn't my boss and could have simply told me she had other priorities. But Christine's priority is putting people first, and she intuitively understood that I had been given a big job that I wasn't sure I could handle. Her message, which I'll never forget, was, "You can do this, and everything will be OK. We are in this together." I got not only the resources I needed to succeed but also emotional support that gave me the confidence to do something beyond my qualifications. The event was a blockbuster, attracting buyers who had over $1 billion to spend and senior officials from tourist destinations. Together we launched what became an annual industry summit.

This may surprise you because my next leadership example pays tribute to my direct competitor, Paul Sarvadi, chairman and CEO at Insperity.[8] Although we might compete deal by deal now, I'm filled with gratitude for the experience I gained at Insperity and for getting to see Paul in action up close from time to time. Paul was a founder of Insperity and led the company from financial insecurity to multibillion-dollar enterprise. Among the many things I learned from Paul was the role senior leaders can play during a difficult business transition.

A program that I was hired into was moving from an incubation phase into being a division of the company, without a clear consensus about its future course. Paul and other senior leaders came to Augusta, Georgia, for a few long days of meetings to figure out where we were headed. Because Paul has a very clear, single-minded vision for the company, he cut through the confusion in a firm but gentle way. He was able to provide structure to the role of the new division. Where we might otherwise have been spinning our wheels, we left ready to move forward because the leadership of the new division and the company were highly aligned. For a

---

8   Paul Sarvadi is the author of *Take Care of Your People: The Enlightened CEO's Guide to Business Success* (Charleston, SC: ForbesBooks, 2019). For more information, visit PaulSarvadi.com.

CEO of a large company, Paul was investing a lot of time in one meeting. But he anticipated all the objections and questions his people had, and he wanted to unpack and explain the issues. His personal commitment to ensure that we started off on the right course paid dividends for years because our mission was clear and we felt invested in and supported. I try to emulate that direction-setting with my own team.

DEALING WITH FAILURE

After reading these success stories, you may be wondering how human-centered leadership deals with abject failure. At some point you may discover that an expensive mistake has been made at your organization—a wasteful procurement, a terrible hire, a major client alienated. I can tell you what happens when a customer comes to me complaining about being let down by someone at my company. It rarely happens, fortunately, so I might be tempted to brush it off as a fluke or a misunderstanding on the client's side.

The more respectful, human response is to say, "Help me understand what happened." I would take the time to get all the details of the story from all the parties involved, including the person named in the complaint. Asking a lot of questions is worth the time because it avoids the risk that someone is left feeling unfairly judged or dismissed. Complaints can be overstated,

> **If you conclude that something terrible happened at your organization solely because one person dropped the ball for no reason other than bad intentions, negligence, or incompetence, you probably are wrong.**

fueled by secondhand gossip. Some complaints are false or less than fully factual. The same concern holds true for all types of stories that work their way up to senior leaders.

If you conclude that something terrible happened at your organization solely because one person dropped the ball for no reason other than bad intentions, negligence, or incompetence, you probably are wrong. Usually there is more going on, a bigger picture worth seeing. Maybe there is a gray area in job descriptions that needs to be clarified. Maybe staffers are stepping up to fill gaps they aren't qualified to fill. Maybe they are not being given adequate time to do the job right. If you just blame a particular person or behavior, you're probably dealing with a symptom and not the root cause. Mistakes sometimes result from several complicated, interrelated things. It's impossible to understand and address the total picture surrounding a lack of performance if you fly off the handle at the first symptom. Human-centered leaders start by extending trust and assuming the good in people, then take the time to get the facts of what actually happened, making them more effective at solving business problems. If they find that an individual fell short of a well-communicated standard, that person must be held accountable, after being given a chance to own the mistake. By starting with the assumption that team members are valued contributors, you can either work through difficulties together or determine more reliably that somebody isn't a fit for the role or the organization.

TRY THIS:
REHEARSE BEFORE DISCIPLINING

When something bad happens and I need to address it with somebody, I rehearse that message over and over in my mind until I can deliver it with an even keel. It's tempting to immediately call the person into my office and scream, "What the hell did you do here?" If I'm that upset, bad feelings will escalate, and we won't accomplish anything. Leaders and team members are dependent on each other. The even keel disciplinary message is more effective because it can lead to a calm discussion of longer-range solutions to root causes of the transgression.

Because human being leadership looks at the whole person, there is more likelihood of seeing potential in people that others might miss. In a tight labor market, there's a strategic advantage to being able to find applicants who can transcend what appears to be a flawed or an insufficient background. We have done very well at Questco hiring up-and-comers because our supportive culture allows them to grow in their roles. They appreciate how we took a chance on them when they didn't have a track record, so they tend to be highly committed and loyal employees.

WORKING WITH FAMILY MEMBERS

Some of us know a whole lot about the background of one type of person we find ourselves in business with: a relative, or a close friend who is almost like a family member. Human-centered leadership encounters specific challenges in this situation. Forget the conventional wisdom that holds you can be friends or family outside of work and just business colleagues at work. The late motivational speaker Zig Ziglar made a career in business coaching offering relationship advice, believing that people are basically the same the world over and that you can't be one person at work and a totally different person at home. "You can't truly be considered successful in your business life if your home life is in shambles," Ziglar said. You are who you are. A family relationship is still a family relationship when you just happen to be at work. Instead of trying to turn off the relationship at the office, it is better to acknowledge it and the challenges it presents. The challenges exist within the relationship itself and in how others in the organization perceive it.

Some CEOs who embrace human-centered leadership speak of their company as being like a family. That's a strained metaphor because families don't have job titles and compensation packages and they can't be hired and fired like employees. But there *are* family businesses that have unique dynamics. I have been exposed to these situations through my work in professional employer organizations, because small family businesses often wisely outsource human resources management.

I've also had the distinct pleasure of working with my brother in a start-up business and my very close lifelong friend, Michael Berger, who is like family to me. In both cases, we established a shared understanding of the boundaries of the relationship at work. Mostly we had to be mindful that our behavior appeared professional to others. In meetings, for example, we had to avoid private jokes. We embraced the positive aspects of our relationship—its stability, our affinity for and trust in each other, and the way we could communicate efficiently. But we made sure that we didn't use shorthand language in a way that excluded others or created an impression that favoritism or nepotism was driving decision-making. I have seen businesses in which a toxic work environment developed when a family member was seen as immune by birthright from responsibility to behave or even dress like others in the office.

As a business leader, you should hold a family member to the same standards of performance, professionalism, and behavior as anybody else. It is impossible to expect employees to trust that you are doing so if you don't overtly acknowledge the relationship and its role in your working together. You have to make clear that any complaints regarding the relative or friend will be treated with professionalism and confidentiality. Family businesses can be even more productive than businesses that don't have family attached, as long there are not two classes of employee. As always in human-centered leadership, the goal is to have employees feel that they are being treated fairly.

A lesson I learned doing physically exhausting work for long hours at the pizza franchise I owned with Michael has stayed with me. Frustrations would build up, and I would yell at him in public in a way I would not have done with somebody who wasn't like a brother. By the time my actual brother, Mike, brought me in to run his business, I had come to understand that professionalism rules the day and that there can be no double standard of behavior for close relationships. The family relationship then became a positive, reassuring thing, having someone who understood me as a total person by my side as our business went through a lot of challenging change. We were giving each other the benefits of human-centered leadership—extending trust, showing humility, offering support. But as for the advice in the previous chapter about spending time and asking questions to better understand those whom you are working with, we could skip that step of really getting to know each other!

JUST BE A HUMAN BEING

We started this chapter with comic book supervillains to show the dangers of cruel, dismissive, and threatening leadership styles and the equally counterproductive best-buddy approach. As I have tried to apply servant leadership in my career, a particular phrase has best expressed what works for me: just be a human being. Don't try to be a CEO superhero; take complaints and deal with mistakes without getting ruffled, and try to fully understand any failures rather than lash out. Exercise authenticity, positivity, humility, structure, and accountability. The stories in this chapter illustrated how leadership using these characteristics helped me, my company, and others get through challenges and difficult transitions and how human-centered leadership could apply to a family business.

It is important to note that the same principles pertain to all business situations, even those that seem insignificant. What starts out small can metastasize quickly and burn its way into collective memories. (You saw how I still remember the boss who almost made me miss a flight home almost twenty years ago.) Feelings of being slighted are driven more by perception than by facts. One bad example can lead to people saying, "I guess that's how it goes here." Senior managers who understand these unfortunate natural tendencies can nip them in the bud by picking up early hints of unspoken complaints and addressing them in a positive way. That's affirming human-centered leadership.

The next chapter deals with an even more proactive principle, establishing clarity of purpose within an organization.

CHAPTER SIX

CLARIFY YOUR PURPOSE

We have looked within ourselves to see how the tremendous responsibility of senior business leadership weighs on us. We saw the dangers of buying into the myth of the CEO superhero, how that myth can only deepen our anxieties and undermine our efforts. We have explored the potential of human-centered leadership and embraced the power of our support system. We have begun to cultivate a spirit of service in our leadership approach. It's time to turn our focus outward.

Having a team by our side gives us the power to transform our organizations. So, we have to ask: What are we going to do with that power? What kind of transformation are we going to pursue, and where will we begin? We'll start with a fictional story, loosely based on one of my consulting experiences, that shows how leadership fails without clarity of purpose.

THE CASE OF THE SHINY OBJECT

I was brought in to help a midsize agency pursue transformative growth. This business had a serious challenge—its services had become increasingly commoditized. It needed to elevate its product to be more bespoke so that more revenue would come from higher-value custom services. That fundamental change presented a clearly defined goal. For some reason, this agency saw the path to its goal as involving the establishment of another business unit as a complement to its existing business. Why would that be?

As I worked with the agency's senior leaders, it became clear that they had another unstated goal. They were really worried about losing two key people. Janet and Bob were the creative minds who came up with the multimillion-dollar ideas that would ensure the agency's success in elevating its product. Janet and Bob were getting bored and looking for something fresh to work on, which meant they could bolt at any time. They had senior roles in the agency, in the sense that they were put on pedestals and not in the sense that they were deeply connected parts of the team. The idea of the separate business unit was all about dangling a shiny object in front of Janet and Bob. They would be promoted to lead a new business.

Retention of key personnel is a sensible goal, but the thought process of this agency's leaders was backward. Instead of starting with an analysis of customer needs, or even the larger company's challenges and potential, the motivation was satisfying a couple of diva-like high performers. This agency had an admirable culture of doing right by its people. Removing Janet and Bob to their own fancy silo would not serve the entire organization well. It would be hard to produce a good spin for the people and customers of the core agency on why their creative inspirations were moved elsewhere. A worst-case scenario could involve Janet and Bob eventually leaving anyway and the new business unit collapsing.

My consulting work focused on the production of a credible business plan for the entire agency—where its revenue might come from, a multiyear scaling model that would yield profitability. My plan did not support the separate business unit because of the human-factor risk it presented. The plan did recognize the important role of Janet and Bob and recommended finding ways to integrate their type of creative spark more widely into the agency. Instead of an isolated, two-person idea shop, the plan was to cultivate and reward creativity throughout the agency. The company would commit to a culture in which the strength of the team as a whole was the focus instead of any one person's exceptional, unique contributions. That decision paid off a couple of years later when Janet and Bob had moved on anyway, in pursuit of an even shinier object.

WHAT KIND OF TRANSFORMATION?

The previous story shows how a muddled sense of purpose could undermine a business transformation. The agency leaders started in a good place, trying to keep a couple of strong performers happy and engaged. But one thing led to another, and they were about to abandon their central mission of being a creative agency full of people with good ideas. There was an echo of the superhero myth in their thinking that two people had the unique ability to drive their desired transformation. Other organizations get sidetracked in many other ways from focusing on their goals.

There are always external and internal pressures on our organizations that test our beliefs in who we are. We have seen how a pandemic can almost instantly transform our economy and force retrenchments. Amid such a catastrophe, an opportunity could spring up to win a very large contract that would fundamentally change the nature of our business. The list of internal and external pressures could go on and on: mergers and acquisitions, changing technology, changing marketplace demand, and demographic changes affecting the clientele or consumer base. Or an important stakeholder within our organizations asks us to make an exception from our regular practices. In these and other cases of external and internal pressures, we must reevaluate our skills, resources, behavior, and overall goals. It's not up to the world to conform to our view of what our company should be. It's up to us to adapt to the events of the day in the context of who we are. We must begin with a firm understanding of who we are, what our organization exists to do, and why that matters. With that understanding, we can look beyond the momentary pressures, no matter how tempting or inevitable they seem, and act wisely, consistent with our values.

We cannot lead a transformation of an organization unless we understand what it is and what it wants to become. We have to ask,

> **We cannot lead a transformation of an organization unless we understand what it is and what it wants to become.**

"What needs to change and how? What would the organization look like if we achieved our goals?" We also need to understand why we are seeking transformation. Truly examining our motivations is the only way to discover whether we have unstated goals at odds with our stated goals, as occurred in the story about the creative agency.

Having some contradictory goals is a common circumstance that must be acknowledged and resolved.

THE LIMITS OF A MISSION STATEMENT

Drafting or reevaluating a mission statement can play a role in clarifying your organization's purpose. But the mission statement must be authentic—true to the culture the organization already has built, or in the case of a start-up, is trying to build. Some people's eyes will roll at the mention of a corporate mission statement. The critics think it's a boardroom exercise in which people detached from the day-to-day reality of a business come up with a high-minded vision of dubious relevance to the daily functioning of the organization and its people. Some mission statements are so generic that they could apply to any organization. Others are too vague and undefined or too glossy. A mission statement also could come off as inauthentic, for example, if a business built around being efficient, lean, and low cost articulates its purpose as being a caring, high-touch partner. Proclaiming a purpose that strikes employees as inconsistent with their firsthand experience can make them cynical and eventually disengaged. Mission must start with something authentic inside an organization and radiate outward. It can be aspirational but not delusional.

Counterintuitively, a mission statement should be controversial. To come up with a distinctive and authentic mission statement, we must ask the question: Would anyone's vision be the opposite? For example, if our mission statement is to do good for the world, what type of organization is going to say its purpose is the opposite, to do bad? We are not talking about the villains in James Bond movies here but corporations with different business models. Some run cost-efficient operations and others spare no expense to dote on customers.

An authentic mission statement describes a way of doing things in which there is room for a different approach. Standing for something is more authentic than standing for everything.

EVALUATING, DIAGNOSING, COMMUNICATING

If you are a newcomer taking over a leadership role, you can bring fresh eyes to the process of clarifying an organization's purpose. But it will be a whirlwind time, and a proper evaluation includes finding out what all types of stakeholders think. A disciplined, high-energy approach is needed to get as much perspective as possible from employees, customers, and suppliers and then reconcile what they say with your own point of view. You'll have to ask a lot of questions and evaluate the usefulness of the answers. You are diagnosing whether the organization has a clearly understood purpose. If you're not hearing anything authentic, unique, and controversial, you have work to do establishing a clear purpose. If you are getting wildly different answers, your organization has lost its sense of purpose, if one in fact existed. Most likely you will hear some things that are not appropriate for the kind of organization you believe you are leading and building. You will begin to understand what has to change and what has to be discarded. The purpose has to be something other than making money or pleasing ownership. You must fundamentally answer a basic question: Why should anyone care whether this company exists?

Once you clarify your organization's authentic purpose, you begin the most fun but challenging part of your job: communicating that purpose. Although you synthesized it from feedback others gave you, they are waiting to hear it from you. Authentically, frequently, and energetically communicating the organization's purpose is central to your leadership and momentum going forward. The communication should be simple, consistent, and nearly constant so that everybody understands how their contribution affects the organization's purpose. This is far easier said than done.

Effective communication doesn't just involve articulating your organization's high-minded ideals, no matter how worthy. Instead, you must spend the necessary time to make sure that everyone understands and buys into how these ideals affect their roles. The understanding of the organization's purpose must be internalized so that your people develop enthusiasm and conviction for it and promote it among their teams. Otherwise, the organization's sense of purpose will erode under the internal and external pressures discussed earlier in this chapter.

PUTTING PURPOSE INTO PRACTICE

Clarifying and communicating the organization's purpose is not a job for only new leaders. Because any pressure from day-to-day operations threatens to move us off our true north, we must be careful stewards of our purpose and adjust constantly in how we build on and communicate it. If the daily pressures have begun to erode the authenticity, uniqueness, and controversy of the stated purpose of the organization, then what? It's very important for leaders to have the judgment to know whether to resist succumbing to the pressures or whether it's time to adapt the purpose to new circumstances and realities. Because an organization's purpose should be something of lasting value, adjustments should be infrequent.

How I put this business philosophy into practice at Questco is instructive because the company had been around for almost thirty years but lacked a clear articulation of its purpose. When I arrived as a new CEO in early 2018 and started talking to the staff, it was clear that our company and its people profoundly cared about the well-being and success of our clients. I found that to be a really compelling cornerstone for a clear statement of purpose. Our clients are business owners dealing with a challenging landscape in which they feel alone and need guidance and support. Showing how we could provide that guidance and support in an exceptionally caring way would add value. The generic mission in our HR outsourcing industry is providing reliable, expert, and efficient service to employers. But our purpose was not to just match the service necessary to compete in our industry. Saying that our purpose was to be a caregiving organization would be authentic, unique, and controversial.

Our business clients' employees become, in certain respects, our employees as well. They contact us about issues that can be sensitive, private, and emotional. When they call to ask about something like medical insurance, we take ownership of the issue, ask questions with empathy to make sure that we understand the situation, and follow through to ensure that they got the right answer. An efficiency-based approach might involve just giving out a medical insurance company phone number for the client to call. The qualitative difference in our approach is only possible because our employees firmly understand that they are there to solve problems, not just answer questions or hand out information and referrals. They are there to handle the emotional aspect of employment service and to be a bolstering resource to keep clients' employees happier and more productive. Their purpose is to be a caregiver.

We have to be similarly responsive to our clients' operations leads, human resources officers, payroll supervisors, and others we interact with regularly at a professional level. They may be calling us with questions about dealing with an emotionally charged situation—for example, workplace harassment. An efficiency-based approach would be to direct them to information in an article or on our website. But no matter how accurate or relevant that information is, it's not the same as our owning the problem and being a caregiver.

SOME CAUTIONARY NOTES

People expect an organization to be qualified to fulfill its stated purpose. Nobody wants to visit a clinic and hear a doctor say, "Hold on, let me google those symptoms and see what I can find out." When we commit at Questco to be caregivers and help solve problems, we have to staff appropriately with people who have the training, background, and certifications to take ownership of issues rather than just giving out referrals and web links.

Purpose doesn't have to mean high touch or involve providing extra service. It means being true to the promise the organization makes to the world. If a retailer's value proposition is providing low prices with a limited selection, it must follow through by being ruthlessly efficient and constraining costs. Maybe it wants to be friendly too, so it hires extra employees to walk around smiling and greeting customers. That inefficient extra service could interfere with the completely valid purpose of serving budget-conscious consumers. If the organization decides to add value by offering goods or services that customers can't afford, the clarity of its message will be lost. It will be stuck in a murky middle spot in which it is not as high touch as the truly high-touch retailers and not as efficient as the truly low-cost providers.

This principle of really knowing your value and selling into it has been explained well in other business books, such as *The Disci-*

pline of Market Leaders by Michael Treacy and Fred Wiersema.[9] In our complex world, organizations generally won't fit perfectly into a neat model laid out in a business book. But being discordant from one's own conception of the organization's purpose inevitably leads to problems.

SOME PRACTICAL TACTICS

Like everything else we've discussed, finding clarity of purpose requires support and cannot be achieved by a CEO superhero working alone. I didn't reach clarity about Questco's purpose from behind my desk but instead by talking with—and listening to—lots of people. Be prepared to have a learning experience. Most leaders probably will start by talking informally with team members and other stakeholders. But depending on how far the organization has strayed from clarity of purpose, a structured effort may be required, including bringing in consultants or other outsiders to offer new perspectives.

Some team members may be flattered or grateful to be asked a lot of questions about what they do, but others will be cautious and suspicious. Here's where the four key attributes discussed in chapter 3 come in. Communicating with simplicity and authenticity about where so many questions are coming from will help defuse anxiety. A transparent process in which the outcome is clearly communicated will generate electricity and infuse accountability into the company culture.

---

9   Michael Treacy and Fred Wiersema, *The Discipline of Market Leaders: Choose Your Customers, Narrow Your Focus, Dominate Your Market* (Boston: Addison-Wesley, 1995).

TRY THIS:
SIX-MONTH FOLLOW-UP

One of my company's board members suggested this routine for a new leader: ask a frontline employee and a more senior executive what the purpose of the company is. Make a note to follow up with both of them six months later but then ask what their purpose is—how they contribute to the success of the company. Seeing how consistent their initial answers are with each other's is a good measure of the company's sense of purpose. But if you want to see how successful you have been at promoting an authentic culture and sense of purpose, look at those follow-up answers. Do they fit with each other and with your message?

Clear communication of the organization's purpose allows employees to see where they fit in so that they can develop and fulfill complementary individual goals. It should be the responsibility of managers throughout an organization, especially if it is large or sprawling, to carry the message about clarity of purpose into staff meetings and individual performance conversations. Being able to have monthly all-company meetings, we start each one with an artic-ulation of our purpose and core values. It's especially important for new employees to hear this message with regularity so that it becomes familiar. But you may be wondering how veteran employees react to hearing the same message every month. They understand that we are not only reinforcing the message itself but also making a statement about the priority that we place on the message. We all are familiar with the power and symbolism of rituals, whether religious, patriotic, or some mantra you adopt to help yourself improve in some way.

If managers can't or don't faithfully articulate the purpose of the organization and how they contribute to it, frontline employees certainly won't be able to. Their goals and performance won't be well aligned with the organization's purpose. Success requires promoting the sense of purpose in every stage of the employee life cycle. While hiring, we ask: Does this candidate embody our purpose? We see Questco as a caregiver, so someone who seems solitary and standoff-ish is probably not going to be a good fit regardless of their skills and credentials. We also emphasize responsiveness, client-centricity, and a collaborative spirit. We customize our job descriptions to reflect those expectations. Similarly, we remain mindful of our purpose during training, evaluations, promotions, and retirement celebrations.

Most companies systematically reward financial achievements, but at Questco we also find ways to celebrate our people for exemplifying our values. Just as we give awards for being the top sales producer, we give an award for being a culture champion. There is no objective performance metric involved, but we solicit feedback from managers on who is personifying the organization's values. We give out a trophy periodically, and it carries a fair amount of prestige because we announce how the winner specifically behaved in a way that promoted the overall business. The trophy doesn't come with a check, but indirectly the recognition can be financially rewarding when factored prominently into periodic performance reviews.

A REALITY CHECK ON EXPECTATIONS

For anyone taking on the stressful challenge of transformational leadership, confidence must be tempered with humility. As we discussed in chapter 2, humility is the powerful link that liberates business leaders from the myth of the CEO superhero. We cannot expect to transform things that are beyond our control. Knowing the limits of our potential impact must inform how we fulfill our purpose.

Best-selling author Shawn Achor has written about the importance psychologically of feeling that our actions have a direct effect. Because small successes can add up to major achievements, Achor suggests in his book *The Happiness Advantage* to take on one small challenge at a time—a narrow *circle of influence* that slowly expands outward.[10] When faced with leading a major transformation, the task can seem overwhelming, and it can be hard to know where to start.

Achor offered a memorable way to remind yourself to start by mastering control within a small circle: the Zorro Circle. It refers to a scene in the 1998 movie *The Mask of Zorro* in which the legendary swashbuckler was learning to swordfight. His mentor taught Zorro to draw a circle in the sand and to focus on controlling that bit of ground before taking on the rest of the world.

> **We cannot expect to transform things that are beyond our control. Knowing the limits of our potential impact must inform how we fulfill our purpose.**

Let's look at how this concept plays out in a business environment. I started the introduction of this book with a story about taking over as CEO of Coast to Coast Tickets, an online business that had no playbook for managing its growth and no road map to success. I didn't even really understand a key part of the business, the dynamic pricing of its ticket inventory for various events at different times and places. I had to have the humility to admit that I needed to focus on gaining a firm understanding of that technical area before I could

---

10   Shawn Achor, *The Happiness Advantage: How a Positive Brain Fuels Success in Work and Life* (New York: Currency, 2010).

have the confidence to make big decisions regarding the company, its purpose, and its people.

In reality, a new company leader must range over a lot of ground, putting out brushfires, pleasing various stakeholders, and fulfilling financial goals. Where we must draw the circle in the sand, to transcend the day-to-day challenges, is that we will focus on something we can do now as a step toward fulfilling the organization's core purpose. That focus does not relieve a leader of broader responsibility for the entirety of the business. It's not an excuse for ignoring everything else, but it is a method of building confidence. Being transparent about the reason for focusing on something is important. A human-centered leader would not let one group within the organization feel that it is going through a deep forensic audit while everyone else is getting a pass.

LIVING LIFE WITH PURPOSE

A well-known study from the 1970s illustrates the impact of feeling control and responsibility for one's daily experiences, no matter how limited your circle of influence. Harvard University psychologist Ellen Langer gave houseplants to two groups of nursing-home residents. One group was responsible for making their own schedules during the day and for keeping the plants alive. The other group was given no choice over their schedules and told that staff would care for the plants. As recounted in the *New York Times Magazine* several years ago, "Eighteen months later, twice as many subjects in the plant-caring, decision-making group were still alive than in the control group."[11]

---

11   Ellen Langer, "Long-Term Effects of a Control-Relevant Intervention with the Institutionalized Aged," *Journal of Personality and Social Psychology* 35, no. 12 (1979): 897–902.

ENJOY THE CLARITY WHILE IT LASTS

Senior leaders have the power to transform our organizations but only if we are smart about how we handle that power. We have to know where to begin, which requires having or creating clarity about our organization's purpose. A muddled sense of purpose could undermine a business transformation. A good starting point is to have a mission statement that is authentic—true to the culture the organization already has built, or in the case of a start-up, is trying to build. A new leader must systematically evaluate whether the organization has a clear purpose and is putting it into practice. Clarifying and communicating the organization's purpose is an ongoing challenge. We have to focus efforts where we can have impact. We cannot predict or control all the internal and external factors that buffet our organization. Change is constant, and that which we control today may be out of our hands tomorrow. How to deal with that volatility is the subject of the next chapter.

CHAPTER SEVEN

FLY IT WHILE YOU BUILD IT

The first law of leadership is that no plan survives contact with reality. When I started at Questco, I had an agenda for my first week. The agenda went out the window on the first day as I encountered one unexpected thing after another. This chapter is about learning to be comfortable with unpredictable and even chaotic developments. You may be surprised to find out where I developed that skill, because it was not in a classroom or an office. But first let's revisit a story I told in chapter 3 about being shocked by the response to my announcement of a bonus plan.

Bonuses at our company had been issued in an ad hoc or discretionary way, and we wanted to make a more formal plan to strengthen the link that flowed from individual behavior to company success to financial reward. Given the amount of money we were committing, we expected the plan to be warmly received. We rolled out the QUIP, for Questco Incentive Plan, with fanfare. But the joke was on us. Many employees had either done well under the old system or had received informal, unwritten promises of more money. In a few cases, we were giving people more responsibility— a promotion with a pay raise—along with a significant increase in their bonus opportunity. I presented them with this good news and was greeted with shocked faces, folded arms, and tears welling up. I was blown away when they said my predecessors had promised them a lot more. For a significant number of employees, our plan did not appear at all to be what we were touting—an unambiguous win for all involved.

I was flabbergasted by the negative, or at best neutral, reaction. I addressed it directly, explaining why I could not fulfill unwritten past promises. I thought the bonus plan was sound and wanted to stick with it in part because it offered clear promises in writing that we could honor. But I obviously needed to quickly change how I was communicating about the plan. First, I needed to listen and ask questions. "Why are you disappointed?" "What were you expecting, and why?" Once I understood the problem, I couldn't realistically change the dollar amounts, but I could adapt my presentation of the plan. I focused on why it was important to the company, why it mattered to our future, and why it was the right thing to do. I could deliver those messages with authenticity. The result was a baseline of integrity and understanding that would not have been possible if all I did was express indignance that they weren't more grateful.

THE BEST OF INTENTIONS

We started this chapter by saying, "The first law of leadership is that no plan survives contact with reality." That's a variation of an adage that has been said in other colorful ways. "No battle plan survives first contact with the enemy" is the rough translation of a famous saying from a nineteenth-century Prussian general. "Everyone has a plan until they get punched in the face," boxer Mike Tyson said. The point is that reality rudely intrudes on everyone's plans. Some people are better than others at accepting reality and dealing with it. The world rewards adaptation, especially in business.

Anyone who has been intimately familiar with a large corporation implementing a transformation or strategic plan knows how many of those beautiful PowerPoint slides dissolved into vapor. For decades experts threw around a statistic that 70 percent of transformations fail. A researcher debunked that number as unsupported, but it's clear that most transformations fall short of their goals to some extent.[12] There's a whole lot of failure to point to in transformative business leadership—including famous cases like New Coke that I don't need to remind you of. Do you remember how several household-name companies went to market overseas with embarrassing translations of their slogans or brand names? Did you know that Kodak was developing digital photography in the 1970s but decided to stick to marketing film? Who remembers Excite, an early search engine company that turned down a chance to buy Google in 1999? My experience in consulting has convinced me that those who can adapt their plans are much better off than those who can conceive perfect-seeming plans.

---

12   Nick Tasler, "Stop Using the Excuse 'Organizational Change Is Hard,'" *Harvard Business Review*, July 19, 2017, https://hbr.org/2017/07/stop-using-the-excuse-organizational-change-is-hard.

An organizational initiative often stumbles because a leader has assumed that everyone wants the same thing. The leader calls in the manager or supervisor selected to lead the initiative and that person turns down the promotion, not wanting more responsibility. Or the key customer who is supposed to be thrilled by some new product feature already has gone in a different direction.

Failed plans often emerge from imperfect human communications. With the best of intentions, the planners try to find out what their clients, customers, or employees want, but they somehow get a partial answer that leads to a misimpression. Starting with very careful listening and some empathy helps to really understand that other person's point of view. That's easier said than done for a leader of a large organization who has a lot of stakeholder sentiment to track. These leaders have mechanisms they can use, such as surveys and focus groups, but what's really important is their commitment to listen and understand. There's a workshop for that.

> **Failed plans often emerge from imperfect human communications.**

THE POWER OF IMPROV COMEDY

When I was studying in Chicago, I became president of my school's improv club. We did some training with the historic Second City improvisational comedy troupe and performed a few shows of our own. I never got particularly good at improv comedy, but the lessons that I learned from it have stuck with me for my entire life. The talents that make someone like Robin Williams or Tina Fey a natural at improv comedy are obviously quite different from what makes a successful CEO. Smart-aleck comebacks, for example, are not usually good boardroom and business meeting tactics. Businesses have turned to improv comedy trainers not to make their executives funny but to improve their confidence, sense of teamwork, and communications.

The first rule in improv is that the performers must build on what they are given so that the scene can move forward. They must be in character, in the moment, listen carefully to what others are saying, and not deny what they are hearing. Whatever their scene partner says, no matter how absurd, they must respond with some variation of "*yes, and ...*" Suppose the premise for the scene is two strangers, each dining alone, waiting to be seated at a restaurant. The first performer tells the other, "It looks like there is only one table left." Answering with denial—"No, I see two tables free"—would not move the scene forward. Answering, "*Yes, and* we could share a table" would advance the sketch. Answering, "*Yes, and* I want that last table for myself" would thicken the plot by introducing conflict. Either way, the first performer must adapt by responding appropriately, just as one would in a business negotiation over a limited resource.

WHAT IS IMPROV COMEDY?

Improv comedy is a theatrical form that's all about creating something from nothing. "Improv" describes the process; "comedy" describes the product. The performers have no script but do have a plan for getting started, usually by taking a suggestion from the audience. Someone in the troupe asks the audience a question, and the answer provides the premise for the scene, whether it is the setting, an emotion, an occupation, an activity, or whatever. The improvisers build a scene, introducing some characters and conflict to make it dramatic and funny. A new piece of theater plays itself out to its logical conclusion.

The action may end when a director cuts it off, lights go out, or the actors exit the stage.

The Second City, which began in a small cabaret in Chicago about sixty years ago, is among the best-known brands in improv-based sketch comedy, with many successful alumni: Alan Arkin, Dan Aykroyd, John Belushi, Steve Carell, John Candy, Stephen Colbert, Chris Farley, Tina Fey, Keegan-Michael Key, Tim Meadows, Bill Murray, Mike Myers, Catherine O'Hara, Gilda Radner, Joan Rivers, Martin Short, and Fred Willard. It now operates and offers classes in multiple venues, including private corporate training.

My favorite improv workshop game was called Eulogy. One person would play the deceased, laid to rest on a table in front of everybody. Actors playing friends and family would file by and offer their recollections. I enjoyed playing the pastor who would have to craft a eulogy from the clues offered by the other players. This challenge taught me to stay present in the moment and to *really* listen so that I could be a part of creating a fuller picture. This learned skill was directly transferable to the daily demands of entrepreneurial leadership, although in our Eulogy game as students, somehow it usually turned out that the person died in a bizarrely tragic and X-rated way.

IMPROV CAN TEACH US SEVERAL LESSONS ABOUT ORGANIZATIONAL LEADERSHIP:

- **First and foremost: Things *will* go wrong.**

  » Improvisers have no illusions that they can control their shows. When we train as an improviser, we're training to find comfort in chaos. That's the whole point of the art form.

  » Every discipline works this way, although few acknowledge it. The reality of life is that things *never* go as planned. There always will be surprises, some rising to the level of crises.

  » If we let these surprises flummox or immobilize us, we're always going to feel like we're out of our depth. To get comfortable as a leader, it's crucial to reframe our understanding of the job. Our job is not to formulate the perfect plan. Our job is to invent a new plan after life shreds our perfect plan.

- **Focus on what's in front of us.**

  » Improvisers are taught to play a scene moment to moment. By focusing on what's in front of them and their immediate response, they stay in character and their reactions remain true to the situation. Or as we have often expressed it in this book, they communicate with authenticity.

  » Because improv is chaotic by design and a scene can lead almost anywhere, there is no point in improv worrying too much about what is next or how the whole show is coming off. If the one thing we can count on is chaos, then it really does us no good to worry about that chaos. As leaders, we have to come to terms with the fact that big-picture, long-term outcomes aren't within our control.

  What we *can* control is what's happening right now.

- **A solution will present itself.**

  » Improvisers feel safe focusing on what's in front of them because experience has taught them that the rest of the show will figure itself out. No matter what problems we foresee, we can always trust that a solution will present itself. And that solution is usually just as surprising to us as it is to the audience.

  » We can't stay sane in corporate leadership unless we internalize that principle. We *will* get through this—even if we don't know how yet. Yes, things look terrible, but we are not doomed to defeat. This optimism allows us to be open to a solution when it presents itself, fearlessly embrace change, and lead transformative business initiatives.

- **The team's got our back.**

  » In improv, the rest of the troupe is the biggest source of chaos. No matter how well we think we know them, they can say and do completely unexpected things. But they are also our biggest source of support. They'll solve problems in ways that we would never think to solve them. When we're stuck doe-eyed in front of the footlights at a loss for words, they'll rush onstage to save us with a brilliant line that moves the scene forward.

  » And, of course, as we've already seen, that's the most important lesson there is to learn about leadership: we can't achieve anything on our own. Let our team guide and support us, as we must do for them in return.

- **Finally, find the funny.**

  » Improv comedy is built on the faith that life is going to crack some pretty good jokes while it's tearing our best-laid plans to shreds.

  » Crisis is absurd. Chaos is hysterical. If we can learn to find the humor, our job satisfaction and quality of life will improve.

NO CUTTING DOWN

Finding the humor in business does not mean wisecracking at the expense of others. Years ago, before I developed the philosophy in this book regarding building up others to promote a supportive team atmosphere, I was at a company plagued with work-culture issues and vendettas. About fifteen of us in leadership roles were herded into a meeting to discuss implementing a 360-degree feedback program, in which performance reviews are not just top down but solicit comments from direct reports, key customers, and vendors. I thought the program was poorly designed and at that company would devolve into an instrument of anonymous backstabbing. The woman who had the misfortune of leading the meeting read from her script: "Ultimately we need to accept that feedback is a gift. And what do you do when someone gives you a gift?" I immediately responded, "Well, if I don't like it, I return it." That was funny and a true reflection of my feelings. But today I would not support such undermining behavior in a business meeting.

In a supportive environment, some pretty dark jokes—gallows humor, self-deprecation—can be a unifier. But senior leaders must be cautious of the power dynamics and never make fun of the dress, appearance, or behavior of subordinates who are not in a position to respond.

ADAPTATION IN BUSINESS

Improvisational skills are powerful in the business world because they combine adaptation with positivity. Adaptation here means approaching unpredictable situations by accepting the limits on our ability to control events and outcomes and being open to changes in plans. We're not infallible or omniscient, so we will face setbacks and crises. Positivity involves a belief that we can overcome adversity with the support of our team. In business, having the ability to improvise is not an excuse to not plan. Planning allows us to be ready to be in the moment, to adapt with positivity to the inevitable surprises and crises. A quick-thinking and well-prepared senior leader might have the first and best solutions but assuming that always will be the case is hubris. We always should be listening and understanding what those around us are saying.

TRY THIS:
ACTIVE LISTENING

Short on time and long on experience, senior leaders are often tempted to cut off conversations with team members who offer unsolicited advice or feedback. It's easy to say, "That won't work" or "I don't have time to listen to the complainers." Onstage in an improv comedy troupe, the actor playing the boss would have to say, "Yes, and how would that work?" or "Yes, and why should I listen to the complainers?" Any time we say to someone, "Yes, I'm listening. Tell me more," we come off as empathetic and supportive.

Most senior leaders know the simple trick of active listening: repeating back or summarizing what we have just heard. But it's easier to say "uh-huh" and return to our own agenda in the conversation. We can try to justify this curt behavior by saying that we are executives, not therapists. But negating the emotions of the people with whom we interact does not produce good outcomes. Making certain that people feel heard encourages loyalty and ensures that the leader is kept well informed. Try active listening and the "yes, and" principle in any conversation—business or social—and watch how much better it goes.

Del Close, who taught and directed many of the comedy improv greats at the Second City in the 1970s and 1980s, compared long-form improvising to building a jumbo jet midflight. But somehow, when we have a passionate, united team by our side, the laws of physics suspend themselves. It really is possible to accomplish the business equivalent of flying a plane while you build it.

MAKING A COURSE CORRECTION

Every corporate initiative that I have experienced has needed major revisions and course corrections to succeed. I'll tell you about one I started that seemed perfectly logical when I outlined it at my first meeting with the Questco board. I got the idea from my daughter's college, which had developed a program specifically aimed at smoothing the first-year experience. An office was devoted to communicating with parents and students about the adjustments and behaviors required for success in that difficult transition when a young person goes off to college.

In Questco's business-to-business environment, the first year of a client's experience is crucial for retention. Although our retention is upward of 90 percent, every client is worth a lot to us, so we want to make sure that their early interactions are positive. They are much less likely to leave after the first year when they have fully bought in to our service and it has become part of their routine. The concept of creating a great first impression is unassailable, but implementation of a program is another thing.

The project whiteboard called for deeper interactions with the client and more double- and triple-checking of our work at key moments, such as running their first payroll or setting up their benefit plans. These enhancements would have been nice if we had the muscle to pull them off, but at the time, we didn't. Listening to the feedback I was getting—essentially that we were putting the cart before the horse—I realized that we had work to do to strengthen our processes before we could pull off this initiative. Earlier in my career, I might have ignored the pushback I was getting from staff and defended the program because it was a good idea (and *my* idea!), and I would have ordered the staff to get with the program. But we pivoted, and I believe that first-year clients still have benefited indirectly. When staying the course is important, business leaders are rewarded for being hard-nosed. But perseverance without adaptation just leads to frustration and failure and ultimately to the disengagement of the team members we rely on for success.

It is easy for leaders to mistake their personal beliefs for the fundamental drivers of their business. You may recall from chapter 1 how my friend Michael and I jumped from a direct-mail marketing business to running a pizza restaurant. We had been selling businesses on the advantages of mailing out coupons, so naturally we did the same with our restaurant. We enjoyed seeing our sales volume pick up, but there were diminishing returns from the discounting. We were reluctant to admit how the coupons were taking a hit on our profits because it's uncomfortable to challenge one's own business philosophy. Being true to our general principles doesn't preclude having the humility and open-mindedness to reexamine our specific business decisions.

OVERCOMING CHAOS

Every business will encounter situations in which adaptation is crucial. In the Houston area, where I am located, Hurricane Harvey caused devastating floods in 2017. After we dealt with the immediate disaster response, making sure that we did what we could for people and clients who were affected, we realized that our busin was going to underperform in Houston during the recovery perio Just as our community pulled together to help out neighbors in a crisis, we had to pull our team together to geographically broaden our sales prospecting and relocate some of our back-office functions.

We improvise a lot in business, and not just in reaction to big natural disasters. Business goals can be undermined by something as vast as a pandemic or as small as a word in a new state tax law that has unforeseen consequences. A common business challenge involves a key executive dying unexpectedly without having

> **Business goals can be undermined by something as vast as a pandemic or as small as a word in a new state tax law that has unforeseen consequences.**

created a strong team or business continuity plan. All these scenarios reinforce the importance of the ideas we have been discussing about a supportive team helping us adapt.

BASIC HUMAN INTERACTIONS

We examined techniques in this chapter for putting our leadership principles to work. Not surprisingly, the techniques involve the basic skills for advancing a conversation: really listening to the other participants, being in the moment, and injecting humor. Beyond business, these principles make life better. We discussed in chapter 5 how human-centered leadership comes down to just being a human being. Showing interest in others, asking questions, and finding points of agreement are useful skills for a sales call or a business negotiation. As senior leaders,

tough messages or bad news, but we can keep
working toward a positive outcome.

edy shows a way that we can react in chaotic situa-
new information is coming at us and we must adapt
th the help of a supportive team. If we can avoid denial
en carefully, with an open mind, solutions will present them-
s. I had another point to make here, but I couldn't come up with
in the moment. That's funny, right? Well, maybe just ironic, but
at least it is not a joke being made at anyone else's expense. Just as in
improv, chaos can't freeze you up; the scene—or the business—must
keep moving forward.

As senior leaders, we are constantly seeing our plans dashed
by unforeseen circumstances, but we carry on by improvising. We
have no choice but to fly the plane while we build it. In other
words, we do what we can in the short term, with the time and
resources available, and hope that we are building something far
greater in the long term. That concept of staying on course toward
a long-term vision is the topic of the next chapter. I'll share my
vision for my company and how it was influenced by some of the
hard-earned lessons I have recounted.

CHAPTER EIGHT

CHARTING YOUR COURSE

Our discussion of how to achieve success by building a supportive team may have called to mind an African proverb: "If you want to go quickly, go alone. If you want to go far, go together." Far be it from me to question the wisdom of a proverb so beautifully and prolifically displayed all over the internet, but it doesn't reflect my business experience. Sometimes we need to go fast *and* far to succeed, and we need to get immediate and continuous buy-in and collaboration from our team. We need to chart a course, communicate it well, and earn the support of others by reaching out, listening, showing gratitude—being a servant leader. If you have read this far, you may be willing to embrace this philosophy but still feel unsure of how to chart and follow your own successful course. I can't know what will work for everyone else in their organizations, but I can share in this chapter what has worked for me and my clients.

At Questco, I charted a course that I could communicate to my team with simple clarity: to look out for our clients, we had to focus first on taking care of ourselves. That is a controversial vision in the sense that somebody could disagree with it. Anytime a business puts resources into its own operation, someone could argue that the time and money could be better spent. Moving into a bigger and better facility, hiring fantastic people, obtaining the latest technology, and providing more training all sound great. But are they expensive indulgences, or do they indirectly but substantially benefit the clients and customers? My answer was that our team's succeeding together in a supportive environment was the key to greater revenue and lasting business success.

In business we don't have the luxury of working on one thing at a time. We can't put our clients on hold while we focus on team building. Nor can we be so focused on our performance with customers and clients that we ignore issues within our team. It is not only possible but necessary to care for the team *and* the customer or client. Doing both at once is a sensible plan, not a conflict.

Everything that I've done that was worthwhile was done as a part of a team. If that statement seems surprising, it is because our society tends to measure a person's worth and status based on individual contributions and achievement. American culture celebrates the individual. Our schools reward individual achievements based on grades and standardized tests. In our politics, we look for "the one" to lead us. Our corporations richly reward anyone held out as a CEO superhero. Yet while individual status is limited by our talents, abilities, and achievements, team success is unlimited.

When I embraced the celebration of the team and not the individual, I felt happier. Having everything on an individual's shoulders is unhealthy. It leads to loneliness, detachment, and a more limited worldview. The enormity of responsibility that senior leaders face can cause some to feel a paralyzing fear that they are being ineffective. It's not lonely at the top when we get there together as a team and can have a shared celebration. My vision for Questco was to bring that joyful feeling of having a supportive team to both our staff and our clients.

> **It's not lonely at the top when we get there together as a team and can have a shared celebration.**

Our mission statement is that we're proudly supporting small businesses and the people who enable their success. Running a small business is really hard. There are a lot of expectations. In an increasingly competitive and fast-paced world, businesses must stay on top of complex laws and regulations. Small business owners need help with that compliance, but also with people issues. Questco has the expertise and infrastructure to provide that help, both day-to-day and in long-range planning. There is no way a small business on its own could obtain the kind of tools and products that a professional employer organization, or PEO, can provide and that they really need to succeed. Outsourcing human resources also allows the owners and executives of small businesses to use their time more effectively by focusing on what they do best. Although PEOs have been around for a few decades, some business owners are not familiar with our industry. We have not done enough to explain the value of our services, which is why I am doing so here.

HOW OUTSOURCED HR WORKS

A professional employer organization becomes the legal employer of record for its client companies. The PEO takes on the burden of handling matters such as payroll, tax withholding, HR technologies, access to medical insurance, and workers' compensation claims. Small business owners and executives don't give up their decision-making authority or their ability to shape their unique company culture, but they leave a lot of time-consuming details to HR experts. The PEO, as a co-employer and not just a service vendor, has skin in the game to take excellent care of its client employees. Outsourced HR provides economies of scale for a whole range of services. A small business with twenty employees that outsources HR enables its employees to get benefits normally available only to companies with hundreds or thousands of employees. People-related costs are typically among the largest line items on the profit and loss statement, so there is a potentially huge financial impact to exploring the advantages of an outsourced HR provider. The outsourced HR concept makes so much sense that it can be hard to understand why a small business would opt to go without such a supportive relationship.

PEOPLE-RELATED ISSUES

I got to know PEOs first as a client running a fast-growing start-up facing thorny human resources issues attendant with growth and change. The peace of mind and added productivity I got from the outsourced HR relationship was so profound that I wanted to be a part of it. After that company was sold to a strategic buyer, I went to work for the PEO. I truly believe that every small business owner should at least take a look at the outsourced HR concept to see if it's right for them. Small business owners we work with at Questco have told us that they felt like a weight was lifted from their shoulders when they partnered with us. We like that analogy but take it a step further: we want them to feel like we are walking alongside them and carrying the pack that got lifted from their shoulders. We want them to feel that they are not alone as they face the tremendous challenges of running a small business. Many of those challenges involve people-related issues such as finding top talent, determining what pay and benefits are competitive in their industry or area, and answering employment questions.

Our expertise at recruiting has allowed us to attract for our clients some amazing employees who were not even out looking for new jobs. Compared with market rates for such recruiting services, our clients get a phenomenal deal. Once these valued employees are in the fold, they must be thoughtfully managed to ensure good retention rates. If their small business has partnered with Questco, they will see that their benefit programs are equal or better compared with what their peers get at more glamorous companies with household names. Meanwhile, they are enjoying the small-shop culture, which can be more human and flexible and provide more of an ability to make a true impact on an organization.

One of the gratifying things about working at Questco is really getting to know our client companies because we are working as partners in fulfilling our shared responsibilities to the employees. Every PEO is responsible for getting client employees paid, processing their benefits, and handling day-to-day transactions. The quality of the PEO relationship really gets tested when something happens beyond the transactional responsibilities. The client company could have a workplace accident or a thorny employee relations issue. Instead of searching for an attorney or soliciting advice from colleagues or friends with limited expertise, our client company executives know they will get expert, individualized support from Questco. We have a can-do spirit that really makes a difference when a company needs support the most.

A DISCOVERY PROCESS

It's important for business owners to partner with the right PEO. It would be easy for me to tell you that my company is the always the best choice, but Questco is not the right fit for every business. No service provider is. To help our prospective client companies figure out what they need, both immediately and down the road, we offer a discovery process. We dig into the specifics, and if we find that we can't meet a prospect's goals, or that we have incompatible approaches, we'll part quickly as friends.

Business owners approach us because of some initial motivation. They typically have some tactical problems to solve. Their insurance costs may have soared, or they may have found that technology alone doesn't fully address their challenges, or their current outsourced HR provider is disappointing them. That is just a conversation starter. There are always other issues they may not acknowledge or appreciate that we can help them with. One reason Questco has a great retention rate with clients is that we are there to mitigate risks they did not realize they faced. When something happens, they appreciate the support they get.

Every company is handling its HR issues somehow, but many never consider outsourcing HR, even as they hire outside accountants and lawyers and contract out their marketing and event planning to agencies. Maybe the company has made pennywise decisions about HR hiring, and a wonderful administrative assistant is the de facto benefits manager. Maybe there is one HR professional at the company trying to handle everything. It is common for HR to get less oversight than comparable categories of company spending. We are often asked, "If I hire Questco, will I have to fire my HR person?" Absolutely not. Our job at Questco is to add bionic powers to the person or small team already handling HR at our client companies. We don't replace our clients' people. We make them dramatically more capable. They make decisions, and we carry them out. They have more time to focus on initiatives that have a positive impact on their company's culture and its financial success.

COST CONTAINMENT AND MORE

When it comes to controlling costs for our client companies, medical insurance is probably the biggest issue. Questco has a relationship with UnitedHealthcare and a master plan that our clients can qualify for. That gives them seamless nationwide coverage with phenomenal plan options and features that many of them could not access on their own. We can also help them contain costs year over year because they become part of a large employee group, posing less concentrated risk for the insurer. But there is more to the relationship than increasing the client's buying power. We meet with our partners at UnitedHealthcare several times a year to talk about how our plans are doing, what our clients are asking for, and how they can provide more value to our clients' people.

A lot of the cost savings we provide to our clients involve the opportunity cost of their people's time. For example, many small businesses have accumulated a variety of software from different buying decisions over the years. Relationships with different vendors have given them incompatible systems for time and attendance, payroll, benefits, and so on. Managing all that complexity is time consuming for employees and supervisors. Getting basic information might take four logons, and it may be impossible for senior leaders to see trends hidden in the data. When Questco takes over the functions, the information is streamlined into cloud software. The client company no longer spends time deciding what HR software needs replacement, updates, or consolidation. They don't need special expertise to enjoy our mostly plug-and-play systems, but if they are a more technologically sophisticated organization, they'll love the affordability of the technology they can get.

Sometimes a client is beholden to an existing vendor relationship. Our competitors might say, "Sorry, it's all or nothing. That insurance broker may have served you well for thirty years, but you have to end that relationship to work with us." We don't take that approach. We believe that we should meet our clients at their comfort level. We should show that we can work well with their preferred partners, carve out those services, and provide value by handling the things that make the most sense for the client to outsource. We spend a lot of time with prospective clients to make sure that it makes business sense to move forward together. Rushing into onboarding a client would not provide the good first impressions we aim for. We want to create an exciting and productive working relationship from day one instead of leaving our clients worried about surviving a difficult transition.

It's not an overstatement to call what we do with our clients exciting. They may start off wary of the commitment it takes just to begin exploring a PEO relationship. We minimize the administrative burden on our clients even in the evaluation process, but we do want to meet with everyone whose job would be impacted by the outsourcing, to address concerns and answer questions. When there is a meeting of the minds with the decision makers, we have seen many business owners' eyes light up as they realize the possibilities.

TRY THIS:
SHARE YOUR STORIES

I have shared my company's stories with you and am inviting you to do likewise. Those of us facing similar leadership challenges don't have to go it alone. We can support each other in a community, whether it is local, national, or global. Some of us already are members of an executive coaching organization or network of entrepreneurs. If you have found one of those peer groups helpful, that's great. If you are still looking for a trusted sounding board, you are welcome to get in touch with me. For more information, to contact our company, or to reach me personally, please visit www.questco.net or my LinkedIn profile at https://www.linkedin.com/in/jason-l-randall-b907652/.

STAYING ON COURSE

I believe that having a supportive team is the key to success and happiness in the difficult and sometimes lonely position of running a small business. After I embraced that philosophy personally as a business leader, it was only natural to use the same concept in charting a course for Questco. Over the past few years, we have transformed our culture to recognize that the team is our most valuable resource. That makes sense, because taking care of teams is our job.

I have told you about several ways that Questco and other PEO providers support the small and medium-size businesses that are our clients. We relieve them of the burden of keeping up with a constantly changing landscape of regulation at the federal, state, and local levels. We help with recruiting directly as well as indirectly by meeting prospective employees' expectations and the competition in terms of benefits. We provide economy of scale in implementing time- and money-saving technology and all kinds of benefits programs, especially medical insurance, which is increasingly costly. And in environments of economic uncertainty, we have the resources to guide our clients through complicated decisions with accuracy, speed, and flexibility.

We know that we are on course and following our simple vision if our clients see us not as just another vendor but as a trusted partner. When those companies face people-related issues or fundamental business challenges, we want them to feel that they have a true ally. We are alongside them through crises, and we are there to celebrate their victories.

NEW VIRUS, SAME PRINCIPLES

S hortly after I finished writing this book, the novel corona-virus discovered in Wuhan, China, began spreading into a global pandemic. I was at lunch with a few of Questco's senior leaders, trying to come to terms with the enormity of what lay ahead. Opinions diverged, as was common in early March 2020, with some colleagues having heard that the virus was an overblown hoax or no worse than the seasonal flu. I was resolute that we were dealing with a potential catastrophe.

"We don't know how bad this will get," I said. "But we do know that if we get out ahead of our clients on this, we will be well able to serve them, and our people will be safe." After a robust discussion, we made a tough decision to waste no time and invest heavily in equipping most of our staff to work from home.

Soon we would find out that we were in a once-a-century event that would put all our business skills and personal adaptability to the test. Nearly six months later, I would look back and realize that I hadn't been with those colleagues face-to-face since that fateful lunch, which would be my last in-person business meal for a long time.

We went back to our headquarters, which straddles a county line in Texas, where we quickly realized that we were going to get conflicting and confusing guidance from authorities. To our south is bustling Houston, where officials would soon issue a stay-at-home order. To our north is fast-growing Montgomery County, which President Trump won by more than fifty percentage points in the 2016 election. The small towns and rural areas near our headquarters—and near our service centers outside Phoenix and Omaha—were slow to be concerned about COVID-19. In fact, the Montgomery County sheriff refused to enforce a mask requirement when the governor of Texas reluctantly ordered it four months later.

We felt the need to follow our own North Star and be independent in our decision-making, erring on the side of safety.

The uncertainty of how to respond to the pandemic was weighing on our clients, and we had to serve them. One of my first thoughts was, "We have a good team for things like this." I found myself relying on the principles I wrote about in this book. I would not try to be a CEO superhero. A support system would get me through the seemingly endless months ahead. Taking care of our own people first, making sure that they had a place to work safely, productively, and without distractions, enabled us to come through for our clients.

Within a week, all our people were set up to work remotely, except for a skeleton crew handling essential tasks such as printing payroll checks. Given the sensitivity of some of our work, it was a stretch for most of our staff to work from home. We had to write new rules, adapt technology, and provide the equipment necessary to secure confidential client information. We used videoconferences and surveys to find out what our dispersed team needed. We had to acknowledge and work on solving problems for employees challenged by difficult personal situations. When your leadership approach involves really getting to know people as individuals and recognizing their humanity, they can be forthcoming about such challenges. We can look back and cherish how we worked together to do what was right for them, for us, and ultimately for our clients.

As our clients awoke to the encroaching reality, they faced torturous decisions and were peppering us with questions at up to ten times the normal rate. The unprecedented nature of the pandemic meant that our team couldn't necessarily provide answers—an uncomfortable situation running counter to our fundamental mission. To communicate in the spirit of the four key attributes introduced in chapter 3 (simplicity, authenticity, electricity, and accountability), we tried something new—putting out videos almost daily to our team to address the uncertainties. We didn't fully know what we were dealing with or how long it would last, but we could still communicate empathy and confidence in each other. Our approach was like the safety warning you get on an airliner about sudden cabin decompression: put on your own oxygen mask before you try to help someone else with theirs.

Soon we were back into our groove of helping clients as they dealt with work-from-home policies, expanded unemployment compensation, providing for the safety of essential workers, and all the rest of the constantly changing requirements. Laws were enacted hastily, such as the one creating forgivable loans in the Paycheck Protection Program (PPP), which turned out to be needed and vital but also confusing and messy. Financial institutions prioritized large corporations with existing loan relationships over many of the small businesses we work with. Many of our clients were under intense pressure because their survival was at stake and they were not getting their loan applications through.

Our chief financial officer, Wendy Katz, began webinars for the clients in which she personally, along with attorneys we have on retainer, helped them understand the evolving legal requirements. She took the initiative to have open office hours to answer questions for clients who had nobody else to turn to when they felt lost on the path to financial assistance. The effort was outside our usual HR scope of responsibility, but it paid off because our clients qualified for PPP loans in greater numbers and earlier than the general business population. As they rebuild on the other side of this crisis, we continue to help them with the complicated recordkeeping and reporting involved in qualifying for loan forgiveness and other issues with reopening.

You might think that a CFO would be more concerned about *our* company's profit and loss statement. Our revenue took a hit, at least in the short term, because we charge clients based on head count, and they were temporarily shrinking their workforces. We were providing exponentially more services than ever without charging extra while absorbing significant technology costs. Still, we felt like we were going in the right direction because we were doing what our company was in business to do, supporting clients in their time of need. Empowering the team to do that, exercising the principles in this book, is something I treasure.

As the crisis continued and the initial relief measures expired, we moved on from our initial focus on making sure that our people felt safe to conveying a sense of hopefulness. With board support, we were able to announce that we would not be furloughing or laying off staff or reducing pay. Conveying our financial strength gave our team the confident, optimistic mindset to show clients old and new that they could rely on us.

We were able to celebrate numerous successes, even in the middle of a pandemic. Our clients have, to date, been more resilient than the typical US business, and our dedicated service providers have been thanked countless times for the support they've provided. This service support has made our company's value to our clients clearer; our most recent client satisfaction rating is five times the industry average. And our sales growth team, inspired by the service team's commitment, signed new accounts every single week for nineteen weeks as we produced a record-setting sales year.

While I am proud of my team for stepping up, I also was very impressed with how the senior leaders of our client companies showed how concerned they were about the health, safety, and welfare of their people. How we deal with monumental challenges like the pandemic can open our eyes to possibilities we never considered and, hopefully, lead to safer workplaces and more successful, resilient businesses.

CONCLUSION

My career as a business leader has had some odd and unique twists and turns that I hope you enjoyed reading about. What I want you to remember, though, is what I learned from my successes and failures. Business leaders must invest in their people financially and emotionally. An organizational culture built on the concept of the supportive team will be stronger and more successful than one built around a CEO superhero. Senior leaders who treasure their support system and embrace the principles of servant leadership will be emotionally prepared for the one thing we can always count on in business: the unexpected.

I introduced you to several individuals whose leadership skills I admired over the years. To learn from role models, we must have the humility to realize that we don't have all the answers. We can learn from all kinds of people, including cruel or heartless bosses and those who make the mistakes of knocking their people down or trying to be everyone's buddy. The best leaders know how to just be human beings. They communicate clearly and compassionately, extend trust, and try when possible to help their people recover from mistakes and failures. We are all fallible and can learn by making mistakes. We should be kind to ourselves and give ourselves some grace in maneuvering through challenges. We should imbue our leadership with what some call a positive psychology approach—focusing on people's strengths and what keeps them happy, showing empathy, and giving others control over their well-being.

Improvisational comedy provided an unlikely source for a lesson in business leadership. Improv actors must deal with uncertainty and react quickly to unexpected situations and characters. They must be in the moment, listening carefully to what others are saying and not denying what they are hearing. They must move the scene forward while inventing its premise. The analogy of building a plane while you fly it applies to improv—and to a fundamental business challenge. We often encounter a situation in which we must maintain a legacy business or system while building something greater at the same time. We never have the luxury of doing one thing at a time. We live and work in a chaotic world, dealing with human beings, and we never have enough time, talent, and resources. But as leaders, we know that we cannot give up but instead must chart a course that makes sense for us and that we can communicate with simplicity and clarity.

Having a supportive team gives us the power to transform our organizations, but it is a daunting responsibility. Leadership fails without clarity of purpose. We must take the time to understand what the central purpose of our organization is or should be. Communicating that message clearly and consistently, we can make fulfilling that purpose central to the organization's goals, strategies, and culture.

I have had the good fortune of leading a business whose central purpose was a perfect match for my business leadership philosophy. Questco supports small businesses and the people who enable their success. Most of the time, we perform routine services such as transmitting payrolls and administering benefits. But we also deal with highly emotional issues involving people's health and well-being in which our performance must be compassionate and effective. To ensure that our clients feel confident and supported, we have to show that we know how to take care of ourselves.

It's a tremendous privilege to be able to share my successes and failures with others as a way of paying forward what my mentors and benefactors have done for me. I'm really interested in hearing other business leaders' stories about how they dealt with issues like the ones we covered in this book. Please share your stories with me, and don't hesitate to contact Questco if you think our services might help you or if you have questions about what we do.

OUR SERVICES

Questco offers award-winning customer service across the United States with offices in Texas, Nebraska, and Arizona. We are standing by to give your business the strength of outsourcing to a nationally recognized certified professional employer organization. Outsourcing human resources through a PEO is a strong option for growing businesses. Since our founding in 1989, Questco has distinguished itself with multiple key factors that help our clients more quickly reach higher levels of success:

Flexibility: While many of our clients use Questco to access a comprehensive set of services, we use a flexible approach to offer you the exact blend of services you need, never forcing our clients into a one-size-fits-all model.

The foundations of our offering—which every client uses—are payroll services and HR services. From there, it's up to you. We can offer access to our group medical plans or administer your current plans. We can offer our insurance brokerage services for medical and workers' compensation, or we can work with your existing providers and relationships toward our shared success. This flexibility helps us deliver the right mix of services for you, at every stage of your business growth cycle.

Can-do spirit: The heart of the Questco culture is an unwavering commitment to serve our clients and their people. You and your team can expect to be treated as one of ours, and we will devote a dedicated team to your success. We will know your names, and you will know ours. We form strong human bonds because of the level of care we provide, and these connections are the basis of our long-standing client relationships. We care about you, and this shows in our unmatched ability to come through for our clients and their employees every day.

A certified professional employer organization: Questco has been named a certified professional employer organization (CPEO) by the United States Internal Revenue Service. To achieve and maintain CPEO certification, Questco must continue to meet IRS requirements, including tax compliance, background reports, experience, financial reporting, and bonding.

CPEO certification provides regulatory and cost certainty for current and potential clients, specifically in the following areas:

- Some wage base tax restarts are eliminated. A CPEO has successor employer status for federal payroll taxes, which means that a business that contracts with a CPEO during the year will not face double taxation on FICA and FUTA.

- Tax liability is clarified. A CPEO is solely liable for the federal employment taxes paid to worksite employees. Once the CPEO invoice that includes these taxes is paid by the client, the IRS can collect these taxes only from the CPEO.

- Tax credit eligibility is continued. A client that uses the services of a CPEO remains eligible for certain specified federal tax credits.

Our CPEO certification removes obstacles to becoming a Questco client and provides lasting peace of mind to all our clients.

The IRS does not endorse any particular certified professional employer organization. For more information on certified professional employer organizations, go to www.irs.gov.

For more information and to contact us, please visit questco.net.

ACKNOWLEDGMENTS

Although it's my name that appears on the cover of this book, a work like this is only possible because of the contributions of many others.

That starts with a fantastic support system at Advantage|ForbesBooks. It's truly been a team effort to enable this first-time author to be ready for publication. Central to the success of this work has been Howard Goldberg, who has consistently added structure and depth to my random thoughts. Howard—thank you for being indispensable to this project, and I'm a better communicator because of you.

I've been immensely blessed over the course of my career to collaborate with—and learn from—exceptional leaders. So many of them are unsung heroes, and it has been an honor to share some of these influences within this written work.

My personal and professional life has never been far from Michael Berger, a man that is as much family as he is friend and colleague. We have shared nearly four decades of friendship and have worked together in three separate organizations. Mike, I'm forever grateful for your intellect and support.

Earlier in my career, I was fortunate to work for and with leaders who gave me support, encouragement, and perhaps most importantly, the freedom to explore and to fail. I continue to be inspired by a group that includes Matt Harris, Scott Bush, Christine Duffy, Megg Withinton, Peg Barton, Stephanie Harris, Jim Ochu, Rick Buer, Brad Carmody, and Charlie Ferbet. Over many energetic conversations—and more than a little laughter—you have made me a better professional.

More recently, I made a dramatic transition from leading an outsourced HR client to working for an outsourced HR organization. A group that includes Kathy Johnson, Keith Simmons, Dan Pierce, Shea Brown, Michelle Mikesell, Sharon Dye, and Mike Cassidy was warmly accepting of me at a time when I really needed it. While only a small fraction of our stories made it into this work, our shared experience is something that I reflect on daily as I work to build an organization that's as special as the one we helped build together.

My current organization, Questco, has been supportive beyond any expectation I could have had. Wendy Katz, our CFO, has been my partner in this effort since my first moment at Questco; her dedication and passion inspires me to be the best version of myself. Our senior leadership team also includes Brandon Hartsaw, Emily Bates, Marcy Plourde, and Derek Carlstrom; I'm so proud of what we have accomplished and so excited about the path in front of us. Thank you for the grace you have shown me as we have pursued this project. Likewise, I'm inspired by our Sales Growth leadership team. Derek Carlstrom, Laura Platero, Shawna Smith, Mark Morter, and Hilary Cooper help keep me sharp and focused as we have completely transformed this part of our organization, with a new sophistication that this book will hopefully support. Our board of directors—Nick Peters, Jon Dries, Scott Daum, Ben August, and Eric Nowlin—have shown me unwavering support and significant patience; it's a profound honor to be co-creators in the next chapter of Questco's story. And that story is brought to life by the 140 (and counting) professionals in our Questco family, who show a dedication to our clients and our company that is humbling and inspiring. You are all superheroes to me.

Of course, my actual family has been my greatest source of strength. My brother, Mike Randall, has also been my business partner; his confidence in me changed the course of my career and brought me my first senior leadership role. This work would not have been possible without our lifetime of brotherhood and decades of professional collaboration. Likewise, my sister-in-law Alison Randall was integral to the early success of the business that we nurtured and grew together. I'm grateful to my mom, Rosie, and the consistent enthusiasm she provides and the interest she shows. My late father, Ron, is never far from my thoughts. A lifelong nurturer, he is greatly missed … and I hope that I do his memory justice in my service of others. My daughter, Jessica, and her partner, Jake, provide endless inspiration as young professionals and wonderful people. They were foremost in my thoughts as I was thinking through the stories that would be most resonant and helpful. And, finally and perhaps most vitally, I am in both endless debt and perpetual gratitude to my wife, Lynn. She provides substance, support, and love when I need it most, and has used her considerable skills to make my work—and me— better. Because of the joy she brings to my life, all the rest is possible.

J ason Randall, a business leader with a gift for inspiring success-ful teams, has a résumé nobody would ever build by design. Jason studied accounting at the University of Missouri-Colum-bia, became a CPA for an international firm, then left to start small franchise businesses with a lifelong friend. After taking time out to earn an MBA at Northwestern University's Kellogg School of Man-agement, Jason plunged into the corporate world at Goldman Sachs and Boston Consulting Group before eventually becoming director of brand marketing for Maritz, a storied B2B company.

In 2005, Jason became CEO of an e-commerce company, where he was introduced to the concept of outsourcing human resources as a client of Insperity. He later joined Insperity, a company with more than $4 billion in revenue, serving as a vice president and managing director. In 2018, Jason was named CEO of Questco, a Houston-area HR outsourcing company known for its can-do spirit and award-win-ning customer service.